One Pot

This edtion published in 2010
LOVE FOOD is an imprint of Parragon Books Ltd

Parragon
Queen Street House
4 Queen Street
Bath BA1 1HE, UK

ISBN: 978-1-4454-2235-0

Printed in Indonesia

Created by Terry Jeavons & Company

Notes for the Reader
This book uses both metric and imperial measurements. Follow the same units of measurement throughout; do not mix metric and imperial. All spoon measurements are level: teaspoons are assumed to be 5 ml, and tablespoons are assumed to be 15 ml. Unless otherwise stated, milk is assumed to be full fat, eggs and individual vegetables are medium, and pepper is freshly ground black pepper.

The times given are an approximate guide only. Preparation times differ according to the techniques used by different people and the cooking times may also vary from those given. Optional ingredients, variations or serving suggestions have not been included in the calculations.

Recipes using raw or very lightly cooked eggs should be avoided by infants, the elderly, pregnant women, convalescents and anyone suffering from an illness. Pregnant and breastfeeding women are advised to avoid eating peanuts and peanut products. Sufferers from nut allergies should be aware that some of the ready-made ingredients used in the recipes in this book may contain nuts. Always check the packaging before use.

One Pot

introduction

The great thing about one-pot cooking is that it makes life easier. Everything goes into one pan or casserole, you don't have to schedule time for cooking accompaniments and there's a lot less to wash up at the end of the meal, especially if you have oven-to-table cookware. However, there are other, less obvious advantages too.

Among the most popular one-pot meals are meal-in-a-bowl soups, stews and casseroles because they are so full of flavour. They are usually made with cheaper cuts of meat, which become meltingly tender during prolonged cooking and often have a greater depth of flavour than the more expensive ones. Including plenty of vegetables

and/or pulses in the dish not only adds flavour and richness, but also helps stretch the meat further, making the meal extremely economical. As a rule, most stews and casseroles don't take long to prepare and once they are

simmering delectably, you can go and do something else or even relax while they cook to perfection. Conveniently, they taste even better if they are cooked in advance and reheated and they also freeze well, so if time is limited it is easy to plan ahead.

Not all one-pot dishes are slow cooked and nor are they invariably hearty stews. Stir-frying – one-wok cooking – is one of the fastest ways of preparing food. It is quick and easy to add variety to the family menu with a Chinese chow mein made in minutes or an Indian or Thai curry that takes only a little longer. If you want to ring the changes further, then try a creamy Italian risotto, a mouth-watering Spanish paella or a Creole-style jambalaya – all delicious one-pot dishes.

Fish and seafood benefit from quick cooking and make terrific one-pot meals, whether griddled, roasted or poached in sauce. Vegetarian dishes also tend to be quite speedy, especially if you use canned beans, which do not require soaking and boiling before use.

meal-in-a-bowl soups

Home-made soups are always welcome and have the added advantage of being incredibly easy to make. A meal-in-a-bowl soup is the perfect choice for a weekend lunch for busy families, especially when lots of different activities mean that family members may be eating at different times. They can also be prepared in advance, making them ideal for a late-night supper after a long and busy day or for informal entertaining.

Soups can be hearty winter warmers or lighter, more summery dishes and may be based on vegetables, meat, poultry or fish. For centuries, cooks around the world have recognized the nutritional and economic value of substantial soups for easy meals, basing them on local ingredients and flavours – from Italian minestrone to American clam chowder.

A meal-in-a-bowl soup is a simple way to ensure healthy eating. Meat, fish or pulses provide protein, while a mix of vegetables – the more colourful the better – supplies vitamins and minerals. Many soups contain rice, noodles, pasta or potatoes – all good sources of slow-release carbohydrates to maintain energy levels. If they don't, just serve them with crusty bread or rolls. You can even ladle the soup over slices of bread in the base of the bowls, as is often done in France and Italy.

chunky vegetable soup

ingredients

SERVES 6

2 carrots, sliced

1 onion, diced

1 garlic clove, crushed

350 g/12 oz new potatoes,
    diced

2 celery sticks, sliced

115 g/4 oz closed-cup
    mushrooms, quartered

400 g/14 oz canned chopped
    tomatoes

600 ml/1 pint vegetable stock

1 bay leaf

1 tsp dried mixed herbs or
    1 tbsp chopped fresh
    mixed herbs

85 g/3 oz sweetcorn kernels,
    frozen or canned, drained

55 g/2 oz green cabbage,
    shredded

pepper

crusty wholemeal or white
    bread rolls, to serve

method

1 Put the carrots, onion, garlic, potatoes, celery, mushrooms, tomatoes and stock into a large saucepan. Stir in the bay leaf and herbs. Bring to the boil, then reduce the heat, cover and simmer for 25 minutes.

2 Add the sweetcorn and cabbage and return to the boil. Reduce the heat, cover and simmer for 5 minutes, or until the vegetables are tender. Remove and discard the bay leaf. Season to taste with pepper.

3 Ladle into warmed bowls and serve at once with crusty bread rolls.

minestrone

ingredients

SERVES 4

2 tbsp olive oil

2 garlic cloves, chopped

2 red onions, chopped

75 g/2³/₄ oz Parma ham,
   sliced

1 red pepper, deseeded and
   chopped

1 orange pepper, deseeded
   and chopped

400 g/14 oz canned chopped
   tomatoes

1 litre/1³/₄ pints vegetable stock

1 celery stick, trimmed and
   sliced

400 g/14 oz canned borlotti
   beans

100 g/3¹/₂ oz green leafy
   cabbage, shredded

75 g/2³/₄ oz frozen peas,
   defrosted

1 tbsp chopped fresh parsley

75 g/2³/₄ oz dried vermicelli

salt and pepper

freshly grated Parmesan
   cheese, to garnish

fresh crusty bread, to serve

method

1 Heat the oil in a large saucepan. Add the garlic, onions and Parma ham and cook over a medium heat, stirring, for 3 minutes, until slightly softened. Add the red and orange peppers and the tomatoes and cook for a further 2 minutes, stirring.

2 Stir in the stock, then add the celery. Drain and add the borlotti beans along with the cabbage, peas and parsley. Season to taste with salt and pepper. Bring to the boil, then lower the heat and simmer for 30 minutes.

3 Add the vermicelli to the pan. Cook for a further 10–12 minutes, or according to the instructions on the packet. Remove from the heat and ladle into serving bowls. Garnish with freshly grated Parmesan and serve with fresh crusty bread.

ribollita

ingredients

SERVES 4

3 tbsp olive oil

2 red onions, roughly
   chopped

3 carrots, sliced

3 celery sticks, roughly
   chopped

3 garlic cloves, chopped

1 tbsp chopped fresh thyme

400 g/14 oz canned
   cannellini beans, drained
   and rinsed

400 g/14 oz canned chopped
   tomatoes

600 ml/1 pint water or
   vegetable stock

2 tbsp chopped fresh parsley

500 g/1 lb 2 oz cavolo nero
   or Savoy cabbage,
   trimmed and sliced

1 small day-old ciabatta loaf,
   torn into small pieces

salt and pepper

extra virgin olive oil, to serve

method

1 Heat the oil in a large saucepan and cook the onions, carrots and celery for 10–15 minutes, stirring frequently. Add the garlic, thyme and salt and pepper to taste. Continue to cook for a further 1–2 minutes, until the vegetables are golden.

2 Add the cannellini beans to the pan and pour in the tomatoes. Add enough of the water to cover the vegetables.

3 Bring to the boil and simmer for 20 minutes. Add the parsley and cavolo nero and cook for a further 5 minutes.

4 Stir in the bread and add a little more water, if needed. The soup should be thick.

5 Taste and adjust the seasoning, if needed. Ladle into warmed serving bowls and serve hot, drizzled with extra virgin olive oil.

vegetable & corn chowder

ingredients

SERVES 4

1 tbsp vegetable oil

1 red onion, diced

1 red pepper, deseeded
and diced

3 garlic cloves, crushed

1 large potato, diced

2 tbsp plain flour

600 ml/1 pint milk

300 ml/10 fl oz vegetable stock

50 g/1³/₄ oz broccoli florets

300 g/10¹/₂ oz canned
sweetcorn, drained

75 g/2³/₄ oz Cheddar cheese,
grated

salt and pepper

1 tbsp chopped fresh
coriander, to garnish

method

1 Heat the oil in a large saucepan. Add the onion, red pepper, garlic and potato and cook over a low heat, stirring frequently, for 2–3 minutes.

2 Stir in the flour and cook, stirring, for 30 seconds. Gradually stir in the milk and stock.

3 Add the broccoli and sweetcorn. Bring the mixture to the boil, stirring constantly, then reduce the heat and simmer for about 20 minutes, or until all the vegetables are tender.

4 Stir in 50 g/1¾ oz of the cheese until it melts.

5 Season to taste with salt and pepper and spoon the chowder into warmed serving bowls. Garnish with the remaining cheese and the coriander and serve.

french onion soup

ingredients

SERVES 6

675 g/1 lb 8 oz onions

3 tbsp olive oil

4 garlic cloves, 3 chopped
    and 1 peeled and halved
    lengthways

1 tsp sugar

2 tsp chopped fresh thyme,
    plus extra sprigs
    to garnish

2 tbsp plain flour

125 ml/4 fl oz dry white wine

2 litres/3^{1}/$_{2}$ pints vegetable
    stock

6 slices of French bread

300 g/10^{1}/$_{2}$ oz Gruyère
    cheese, grated

method

1 Thinly slice the onions. Heat the oil in a large heavy-based saucepan, then add the onions and cook, stirring occasionally, for 10 minutes, until they are just beginning to brown. Stir in the chopped garlic, sugar and thyme, then reduce the heat and cook, stirring occasionally, for 30 minutes, or until the onions are
golden brown.

2 Sprinkle in the flour and cook, stirring, for 1–2 minutes. Stir in the wine. Gradually stir in the stock and bring to the boil, skimming off any scum that rises to the surface, then reduce the heat and simmer for 45 minutes.

3 Meanwhile, preheat the grill to medium. Toast the bread on both sides under the grill. Rub the toast with the cut sides of the halved garlic clove.

4 Ladle the soup into 6 flameproof bowls set on a baking sheet. Float a piece of toast in each bowl and divide the grated cheese among them. Place under the preheated grill for 2–3 minutes, or until the cheese has just melted. Garnish with thyme sprigs and serve.

leek & potato soup

ingredients

SERVES 4–6

55 g/2 oz butter

1 onion, chopped

3 leeks, sliced

225 g/8 oz potatoes, cut into
2-cm/^{3}/$_4$-inch cubes

850 ml/1^1/$_2$ pints vegetable
stock

salt and pepper

150 ml/5 fl oz single cream,
to serve (optional)

2 tbsp snipped fresh chives,
to garnish

method

1 Melt the butter in a large saucepan over a medium heat, add the onion, leeks and potatoes and sauté gently for 2–3 minutes, until soft but not brown. Pour in the stock, bring to the boil, then reduce the heat and simmer, covered, for 15 minutes.

2 Transfer the mixture to a food processor or blender and process until smooth. Return to the rinsed-out saucepan.

3 Heat the soup, season to taste with salt and pepper and serve in warmed bowls, swirled with the cream, if using, and garnished with chives.

borscht

ingredients

SERVES 6

1 onion

55 g/2 oz butter

350 g/12 oz raw beetroot,
    cut into thin batons, and
    1 raw beetroot, grated

1 carrot, cut into thin batons

3 celery sticks, thinly sliced

2 tomatoes, peeled, deseeded
    and chopped

1.4 litres/2^1/$_2$ pints vegetable
    stock

1 tbsp white wine vinegar

1 tbsp sugar

2 tbsp snipped fresh dill

115 g/4 oz white cabbage,
    shredded

salt and pepper

150 ml/5 fl oz soured cream,
    to garnish

crusty bread, to serve

method

1 Slice the onion into rings. Melt the butter in a large heavy-based saucepan. Add the onion and cook over a low heat, stirring occasionally, for 3–5 minutes, or until softened. Add the beetroot batons, carrot, celery and tomatoes and cook, stirring frequently, for 4–5 minutes.

2 Add the stock, vinegar, sugar and 1 tablespoon of the snipped dill to the saucepan. Season to taste with salt and pepper. Bring to the boil, reduce the heat and simmer for 35–40 minutes, or until the vegetables are tender.

3 Stir in the cabbage, cover and simmer for 10 minutes. Stir in the grated beetroot, with any juices, and cook for a further 10 minutes.

4 Ladle into warmed bowls. Garnish with a spoonful of soured cream and the remaining dill and serve with crusty bread.

beef & vegetable soup

ingredients

SERVES 4

55 g/2 oz pearl barley

1.2 litres/2 pints beef stock

1 tsp dried mixed herbs

225 g/8 oz lean rump or
  sirloin beef

1 large carrot, diced

1 leek, shredded

1 onion, chopped

2 celery sticks, sliced

salt and pepper

2 tbsp chopped fresh parsley,
  to garnish

method

1 Place the pearl barley in a large saucepan. Pour over the stock and add the mixed herbs. Bring to the boil, cover and simmer gently over a low heat for 10 minutes.

2 Meanwhile, trim any fat from the beef and cut the meat into thin strips.

3 Skim away any scum that has risen to the top of the stock with a flat ladle.

4 Add the beef, carrot, leek, onion and celery to the pan. Bring back to the boil, cover and simmer for about 1 hour, or until the pearl barley, beef and vegetables are just tender.

5 Skim away any remaining scum that has risen to the top of the soup with a flat ladle. Blot the surface with absorbent kitchen paper to remove any fat. Season to taste with salt and pepper.

6 Ladle the soup into warmed bowls, garnish with chopped parsley and serve hot.

mexican-style beef & rice soup

ingredients

SERVES 4

3 tbsp olive oil

500 g/1 lb 2 oz boneless
stewing beef, cut into
2.5-cm/1-inch pieces

1 onion, finely chopped

1 green pepper, cored,
deseeded and finely
chopped

1 small fresh red chilli,
deseeded and finely
chopped

2 garlic cloves, finely chopped

1 carrot, finely chopped

$1/4$ tsp ground coriander

$1/4$ tsp ground cumin

$1/8$ tsp ground cinnamon

$1/4$ tsp dried oregano

1 bay leaf

grated rind of $1/2$ orange

400 g/14 oz canned chopped
tomatoes

1.2 litres/2 pints beef stock

150 ml/5 fl oz red wine

50 g/1$3/4$ oz long-grain white
rice

25 g/1 oz raisins

15 g/$1/2$ oz plain chocolate,
melted

chopped fresh coriander,
to garnish

method

1 Heat half the oil in a large saucepan over a medium–high heat. Add the meat in one layer and cook until well browned, turning to colour all sides. Using a slotted spoon, transfer the meat to a plate. Drain off the oil and wipe out the pan with kitchen paper.

2 Heat the remaining oil in the saucepan over a medium heat. Add the onion, cover and cook for about 3 minutes, stirring occasionally, until just softened. Add the green pepper, chilli, garlic and carrot, and continue cooking, covered, for 3 minutes.

3 Add the ground coriander, cumin, cinnamon, oregano, bay leaf and orange rind. Stir in the tomatoes and stock, along with the beef and wine. Bring almost to the boil and when the mixture begins to bubble, reduce the heat to low. Cover and simmer gently, stirring occasionally, for about 1 hour, until the meat is tender.

4 Stir in the rice, raisins and chocolate, and continue cooking, stirring occasionally, for about 30 minutes, until the rice is tender.

5 Ladle into warmed bowls and garnish with chopped coriander.

spicy lamb soup with chickpeas & courgettes

ingredients

SERVES 4–6

1–2 tbsp olive oil

450 g/1 lb lean boneless lamb, such as shoulder or neck fillet, trimmed of fat and cut into 1-cm/$^{1}/_{2}$-inch cubes

1 onion, finely chopped

2–3 garlic cloves, crushed

1.2 litres/2 pints water

400 g/14 oz canned chopped tomatoes

1 bay leaf

$^{1}/_{2}$ tsp dried thyme

$^{1}/_{2}$ tsp dried oregano

$^{1}/_{8}$ tsp ground cinnamon

$^{1}/_{4}$ tsp ground cumin

$^{1}/_{4}$ tsp ground turmeric

1 tsp harissa, or more to taste

400 g/14 oz canned chickpeas, rinsed and drained

1 carrot, diced

1 potato, diced

1 courgette, quartered lengthways and sliced

100 g/3$^{1}/_{2}$ oz fresh or defrosted frozen green peas

fresh mint sprigs, to garnish

method

1 Heat 1 tablespoon of the oil in a large saucepan or cast-iron casserole over a medium–high heat. Add the lamb, in batches if necessary to avoid crowding the pan, and cook until evenly browned on all sides, adding a little more oil if needed. Remove the meat with a slotted spoon when browned.

2 Reduce the heat and add the onion and garlic to the pan. Cook, stirring frequently, for 1–2 minutes.

3 Add the water and return all the meat to the pan. Bring just to the boil and skim off any scum that rises to the surface. Reduce the heat and stir in the tomatoes, bay leaf, thyme, oregano, cinnamon, cumin, turmeric and harissa. Simmer for about 1 hour, or until the meat is very tender. Discard the bay leaf.

4 Stir in the chickpeas, carrot and potato and simmer for 15 minutes. Add the courgette and peas and continue simmering for 15–20 minutes, or until all the vegetables are tender.

5 Adjust the seasoning, adding more harissa, if desired. Ladle the soup into warmed bowls and garnish with mint sprigs.

scotch broth

ingredients

SERVES 6-8

700 g/1 lb 9 oz neck of lamb

1.7 litres/3 pints water

55 g/2 oz pearl barley

2 onions, chopped

3 small turnips, diced

3 carrots, peeled and thinly
    sliced

2 celery sticks, sliced

2 leeks, sliced

1 garlic clove, finely chopped

salt and pepper

2 tbsp chopped fresh parsley,
    to garnish

method

1 Cut the meat into small pieces, removing as much fat as possible. Put into a large saucepan and cover with the water. Bring to the boil over a medium heat and skim off any scum that appears.

2 Add the pearl barley, reduce the heat and cook gently, covered, for 1 hour.

3 Add the prepared vegetables and garlic and season well with salt and pepper. Continue to cook for a further hour. Remove from the heat and allow to cool slightly.

4 Remove the meat from the saucepan using a slotted spoon and strip the meat from the bones. Discard the bones and any fat or gristle. Place the meat back in the saucepan and leave to cool thoroughly, then refrigerate overnight.

5 Scrape the solidified fat off the surface of the soup. Reheat, season to taste with salt and pepper and serve piping hot, garnished with the parsley.

pork chilli soup

ingredients

SERVES 4

2 tsp olive oil

500 g/1 lb 2 oz lean minced pork

1 onion, finely chopped

1 celery stick, finely chopped

1 red or green pepper, cored, deseeded and finely chopped

2–3 garlic cloves, finely chopped

400 g/14 oz canned chopped tomatoes

3 tbsp tomato purée

450 ml/16 fl oz chicken or meat stock

$1/8$ tsp ground coriander

$1/8$ tsp ground cumin

$1/4$ tsp dried oregano

1 tsp mild chilli powder, or to taste

salt and pepper

chopped fresh coriander leaves, to garnish

soured cream, to serve

method

1 Heat the oil in a large saucepan over a medium–high heat. Add the pork, season to taste with salt and pepper, and cook until no longer pink, stirring frequently. Reduce the heat to medium and add the onion, celery, red pepper and garlic. Cover and continue cooking for 5 minutes, stirring occasionally, until the onion is softened.

2 Add the tomatoes, tomato purée and stock. Add the ground coriander, cumin, oregano and chilli powder. Stir the ingredients in to combine well.

3 Bring just to the boil, reduce the heat to low, cover and simmer for 30–40 minutes, until all the vegetables are very tender. Taste and adjust the seasoning, adding more chilli powder if you like it hotter.

4 Ladle the chilli into warmed bowls and sprinkle with chopped coriander. Pass the soured cream separately, or top each serving with a spoonful.

chicken-noodle soup

ingredients

SERVES 4–6

2 skinless chicken breasts

2 litres/3^1/$_2$ pints water

1 onion, unpeeled, cut in half

1 large garlic clove, cut in half

1-cm/^{1}/$_2$-inch piece fresh
    ginger, peeled and sliced

4 black peppercorns, lightly
    crushed

4 cloves

2 star anise

1 carrot, peeled

1 celery stick, chopped

100 g/3^1/$_2$ oz baby corn,
    cut in half lengthways
    and chopped

2 spring onions, finely
    shredded

115 g/4 oz dried rice
    vermicelli noodles

salt and pepper

method

1 Put the chicken breasts and water in a saucepan over a high heat and bring to the boil. Lower the heat to its lowest setting and simmer, skimming the surface until no more scum rises.

2 Add the onion, garlic, ginger, peppercorns, cloves, star anise and a pinch of salt, and continue to simmer for 20 minutes, or until the chicken is tender and cooked through.

3 Meanwhile, grate the carrot along its length on the coarse side of a grater so you get long, thin strips.

4 Strain the chicken, reserving about 1.2 litres/2 pints stock, but discarding any flavouring solids. (At this point you can leave the stock to cool and refrigerate overnight, so any fat solidifies and can be lifted off and discarded.) Return the stock to the rinsed-out saucepan with the carrot, celery, baby corn and spring onions and bring to the boil. Boil until the baby corn are almost tender, then add the noodles and continue boiling for 2 minutes.

5 Meanwhile, chop the chicken and add to the pan and continue cooking for a further minute, until the chicken is re-heated and the noodles are soft. Season to taste with salt and pepper, then divide among warmed bowls and serve.

chicken gumbo soup

ingredients

SERVES 6

2 tbsp olive oil

4 tbsp plain flour

1 onion, finely chopped

1 small green pepper,
	deseeded and finely
	chopped

1 celery stick, finely chopped

1.2 litres/2 pints chicken stock

400 g/14 oz canned chopped
	tomatoes

3 garlic cloves, finely chopped
	or crushed

125 g/4^{1}/$_{2}$ oz okra, stems
	removed, cut into
	5 mm/^{1}/$_{4}$ inch thick slices

50 g/1^{3}/$_{4}$ oz white rice

200 g/7 oz cooked chicken,
	cubed

115 g/4 oz cooked garlic
	sausage, sliced or cubed

salt and pepper

method

1 Heat the oil in a large heavy-based saucepan over a low–medium heat and stir in the flour. Cook for about 15 minutes, stirring occasionally, until the mixture is a rich golden brown.

2 Add the onion, green pepper and celery and continue cooking for about 10 minutes, until the onion softens.

3 Slowly pour in the stock and bring to the boil, stirring well and scraping the bottom of the pan to mix in the flour. Remove the pan from the heat.

4 Add the tomatoes and garlic. Stir in the okra and rice and season to taste with salt and pepper. Reduce the heat, cover and simmer for 20 minutes, or until the okra is tender.

5 Add the chicken and sausage and continue simmering for about 10 minutes. Taste and adjust the seasoning, if necessary, and ladle into warmed bowls to serve.

turkey & lentil soup

ingredients

SERVES 4

1 tbsp olive oil

1 garlic clove, chopped

1 large onion, chopped

200 g/7 oz mushrooms, sliced

1 red pepper, deseeded and
    chopped

6 tomatoes, skinned,
    deseeded and chopped

1.2 litres/2 pints chicken stock

150 ml/5 fl oz red wine

85 g/3 oz cauliflower florets

1 carrot, peeled and chopped

200 g/7 oz red lentils

350 g/12 oz cooked turkey
    meat, chopped

1 courgette, trimmed and
    chopped

1 tbsp shredded fresh basil,
    plus extra leaves
    to garnish

salt and pepper

thick slices of fresh crusty
    bread, to serve

method

1 Heat the oil in a large saucepan. Add the garlic and onion and cook over a medium heat, stirring, for 3 minutes, until slightly softened. Add the mushrooms, red pepper and tomatoes and cook for a further 5 minutes, stirring.

2 Pour in the stock and red wine, then add the cauliflower, carrot and red lentils. Season to taste with salt and pepper. Bring to the boil, then lower the heat and simmer the soup gently for 25 minutes, until the vegetables are tender and cooked through.

3 Add the turkey and courgette to the pan and cook for 10 minutes. Stir in the shredded basil and cook for a further 5 minutes, then remove from the heat and ladle into serving bowls. Garnish with basil leaves and serve with fresh crusty bread.

bouillabaisse

ingredients

SERVES 4

200 g/7 oz live mussels
100 ml/3^1/2 fl oz olive oil
3 garlic cloves, chopped
2 onions, chopped
2 tomatoes, deseeded and
    chopped
700 ml/1^1/4 pints fish stock
400 ml/14 fl oz white wine
1 bay leaf
pinch of saffron threads
2 tbsp chopped fresh basil
2 tbsp chopped fresh parsley
250 g/9 oz snapper or
    monkfish fillets
250 g/9 oz haddock fillets,
    skinned
200 g/7 oz prawns, peeled
    and deveined
100 g/3^1/2 oz scallops
salt and pepper
fresh baguettes, to serve

method

1 Soak the mussels in lightly salted water for 10 minutes. Scrub the shells under cold running water and pull off any beards. Discard any mussels with broken shells and any that refuse to close when tapped. Put the rest into a large pan with a little water, bring to the boil and cook over a high heat for 4 minutes. Transfer the cooked mussels to a bowl, discarding any that remain closed, and reserve. Wipe out the pan with kitchen paper.

2 Heat the oil in the pan over a medium heat. Add the garlic and onions and cook, stirring, for 3 minutes. Stir in the tomatoes, stock, wine, bay leaf, saffron and herbs. Bring to the boil, reduce the heat, cover and simmer for 30 minutes.

3 When the tomato mixture is cooked, rinse the fish fillets, pat dry and cut into chunks. Add to the pan and simmer for 5 minutes. Add the reserved mussels, the prawns and scallops and season to taste with salt and pepper. Cook for 3 minutes, until the fish is cooked through.

4 Remove from the heat, discard the bay leaf and ladle into serving bowls. Serve with fresh baguettes.

laksa

ingredients

SERVES 4

1 tbsp sunflower oil

2–3 garlic cloves, cut into
    thin slivers

1–2 fresh red Thai chillies,
    deseeded and sliced

2 lemon grass stalks, outer
    leaves removed, chopped

2.5-cm/1-inch piece fresh
    ginger, grated

1.2 litres/2 pints fish or
    vegetable stock

350 g/12 oz large raw prawns,
    peeled and deveined

115 g/4 oz shiitake
    mushrooms, sliced

1 large carrot, grated

55 g/2 oz dried egg noodles
    (optional)

1–2 tsp Thai fish sauce

1 tbsp chopped fresh
    coriander, plus extra
    sprigs to garnish

method

1 Heat the oil in a large saucepan over a medium heat, add the garlic, chillies, lemon grass and ginger and cook for 5 minutes, stirring frequently. Add the stock and bring to the boil, then reduce the heat and simmer for 5 minutes.

2 Stir in the prawns, mushrooms and carrot. If using the egg noodles, break into short lengths, add to the saucepan and simmer for a further 5 minutes, or until the prawns have turned pink and the noodles are tender.

3 Stir in the Thai fish sauce and coriander and heat through for a further minute before serving, garnished with coriander sprigs.

seafood chowder

ingredients

SERVES 6

1 kg/2 lb 4 oz live mussels,
   scrubbed and debearded
4 tbsp plain flour
1.5 litres/2^3/$_4$ pints fish stock
1 tbsp butter
1 large onion, finely chopped
350 g/12 oz skinless white
   fish fillets, such as cod,
   sole or haddock
200 g/7 oz cooked or raw
   peeled prawns
300 ml/10 fl oz whipping
   cream or double cream
salt and pepper
snipped fresh dill, to garnish

method

1 Discard any mussels with broken shells and any that refuse to close when tapped. Put the mussels in a large heavy-based saucepan. Cover tightly and cook over a high heat for about 4 minutes, or until the mussels open, shaking the pan occasionally. Discard any that remain closed. When cool enough to handle, remove the mussels from the shells, adding any additional juices to the cooking liquid. Strain the cooking liquid through a muslin-lined sieve and reserve.

2 Put the flour in a bowl and slowly whisk in enough of the stock to make a thick paste. Whisk in a little more stock to make a smooth liquid.

3 Melt the butter in a heavy-based saucepan over a low–medium heat. Add the onion, cover and cook for about 5 minutes, stirring frequently, until it softens. Add the remaining stock and bring to the boil. Slowly whisk in the flour mixture and bring back to the boil, whisking constantly. Add the mussel cooking liquid. Season to taste with salt, if needed, and pepper. Reduce the heat and simmer, partially covered, for 15 minutes.

4 Add the fish and the reserved mussels and continue simmering, stirring occasionally, for about 5 minutes, or until the fish is cooked.

5 Stir in the prawns and cream. Simmer for a few minutes longer to heat through. Ladle into warmed bowls, sprinkle with dill and serve.

clam & corn chowder

ingredients

SERVES 4

4 tsp butter

1 large onion, finely chopped

1 small carrot, finely diced

3 tbsp plain flour

300 ml/10 fl oz fish stock

200 ml/7 fl oz water

450 g/1 lb potatoes, diced

125 g/4 oz cooked or
    defrosted frozen sweetcorn

450 ml/16 fl oz full-fat milk

280 g/10 oz canned clams,
    drained and rinsed

salt and pepper

chopped fresh parsley,
    to garnish

method

1 Melt the butter in a large saucepan over a low–medium heat. Add the onion and carrot and cook for 3–4 minutes, stirring frequently, until the onion is softened. Stir in the flour and continue cooking for 2 minutes.

2 Slowly add about half the stock and stir well, scraping the bottom of the pan to mix in the flour. Pour in the remaining stock and the water and bring just to the boil, stirring.

3 Add the potatoes, sweetcorn and milk and stir to combine. Reduce the heat and simmer gently, partially covered, for about 20 minutes, stirring occasionally, until all the vegetables are tender.

4 Chop the clams, if large. Stir in the clams and continue cooking for about 5 minutes, until heated through. Taste and adjust the seasoning, if needed.

5 Ladle the soup into bowls and sprinkle with parsley.

meat

Returning home on a cold day to the enticing aroma of a gently simmering stew is one of life's great pleasures, superseded only by sitting down to eat it. Whether succulent beef braised in wine and herbs, a fragrant stew of tender lamb and spices or a heart-warming mixture of pork and colourful vegetables, slow-cooked one-pot dishes are full of flavour and substantial enough to satisfy the heartiest appetite. Not only are these great family meals, but they are also perfect for easy entertaining. The same, of course, is true of pot roasts, which have all the flavour and variety of oven-roasted meat, but are far less bother to cook and much less time-consuming to clear up. What's more, you can guarantee that a pot roast will be moist and tender.

There isn't always time to cook a casserole and stews may be too heavy for summer suppers, but there are still easy one-pot dishes for family meals. You could make a fabulous Thai curry in less than 15 minutes or a classic creamy stroganoff in only half an hour. With recipes inspired by cuisines from across the globe, you are sure to find a whole range of delicious one-pot dishes destined to become family favourites.

beef pot roast with potatoes & dill

ingredients

SERVES 6

2¹/₂ tbsp plain flour

1 tsp salt

¹/₄ tsp pepper

1 rolled brisket joint, weighing
    1.6 kg/3 lb 8 oz

2 tbsp vegetable oil

2 tbsp butter

1 onion, finely chopped

2 celery sticks, diced

2 carrots, peeled and diced

1 tsp dill seed

1 tsp dried thyme or oregano

350 ml/12 fl oz red wine

150–225 ml/5–8 fl oz beef
    stock

4–5 potatoes, cut into large
    chunks and boiled until
    just tender

2 tbsp chopped fresh dill,
    to serve

method

1 Preheat the oven to 140°C/275°F/Gas Mark 1. Mix 2 tablespoons of the flour with the salt and pepper in a shallow dish. Dip the meat to coat. Heat the oil in a flameproof casserole and brown the meat all over. Transfer to a plate.

2 Add half the butter to the casserole and cook the onion, celery, carrots, dill seed and thyme for 5 minutes. Return the meat and juices to the casserole.

3 Pour in the wine and enough stock to reach one third of the way up the meat. Bring to the boil, cover and cook in the oven for 2 hours, turning the meat every 30 minutes. Add the potatoes to the casserole with a little more stock, if necessary, and return to the oven for a further hour.

4 When ready, transfer the meat and potatoes to a warmed serving dish. Strain the cooking liquid to remove any solids, then return the liquid to the casserole.

5 Mix the remaining butter and flour to a paste. Bring the cooking liquid to the boil. Whisk in small pieces of the flour and butter paste, whisking constantly until the sauce is smooth. Pour the sauce over the meat and potatoes. Sprinkle with the fresh dill to serve.

beef in beer with herb dumplings

ingredients

SERVES 6

2 tbsp sunflower oil

2 large onions, thinly sliced

8 carrots, sliced

4 tbsp plain flour

1.25 kg/2 lb 12 oz stewing
     steak, cut into cubes

425 ml/15 fl oz stout

2 tsp muscovado sugar

2 bay leaves

1 tbsp chopped fresh thyme

salt and pepper

herb dumplings

115 g/4 oz self-raising flour

pinch of salt

55 g/2 oz shredded suet

2 tbsp chopped fresh parsley,
     plus extra to garnish

about 4 tbsp water

method

1 Preheat the oven to 160°C/325°F/Gas Mark 3. Heat the oil in a flameproof casserole. Add the onions and carrots and cook over a low heat, stirring occasionally, for 5 minutes, or until the onions are softened. Meanwhile, place the flour in a polythene bag and season to taste with salt and pepper. Add the stewing steak to the bag, tie the top and shake well to coat. Do this in batches, if necessary.

2 Remove the vegetables from the casserole with a slotted spoon and reserve. Add the stewing steak to the casserole, in batches, and cook, stirring frequently, until browned all over. Return all the meat and the vegetables to the casserole and sprinkle in any remaining seasoned flour. Pour in the stout and add the sugar, bay leaves and thyme. Bring to the boil, cover and transfer to the preheated oven to bake for 1³/4 hours.

3 To make the herb dumplings, sift the flour and salt into a bowl. Stir in the suet and parsley and add enough of the water to make a soft dough. Shape into small balls between the palms of your hands. Add to the casserole and return to the oven for 30 minutes.

4 Remove and discard the bay leaves. Serve immediately, sprinkled with chopped parsley.

daube of beef

ingredients

SERVES 6

350 ml/12 fl oz dry white wine

2 tbsp brandy

1 tbsp white wine vinegar

4 shallots, sliced

4 carrots, sliced

1 garlic clove, finely chopped

6 black peppercorns

4 fresh thyme sprigs

1 fresh rosemary sprig

2 fresh parsley sprigs, plus
    extra to garnish

1 bay leaf

750 g/1 lb 10 oz beef topside,
    cut into 2.5-cm/1-inch
    cubes

1–2 tbsp olive oil

800 g/1 lb 12 oz canned
    chopped tomatoes

225 g/8 oz mushrooms, sliced

strip of finely pared orange
    rind

55 g/2 oz Bayonne ham,
    cut into strips

12 black olives

salt

method

1 Combine the wine, brandy, vinegar, shallots, carrots, garlic, peppercorns, thyme, rosemary, parsley and bay leaf, and season to taste with salt. Add the beef, stirring to coat, then cover with clingfilm and leave in the refrigerator to marinate for 8 hours, or overnight.

2 Preheat the oven to 150°C/300°F/Gas Mark 2. Drain the beef, reserving the marinade, and pat dry on kitchen paper. Heat 1 tablespoon of the oil in a large flameproof casserole. Add the beef in batches and cook over a medium heat, stirring, for 3–4 minutes, or until browned, adding more oil, if necessary. Using a slotted spoon, transfer each batch to a plate. Brown the remaining beef, adding more oil, if necessary.

3 Return all of the beef to the casserole and add the tomatoes and their juices, mushrooms and orange rind. Sieve the reserved marinade into the casserole. Bring to the boil, cover and cook in the preheated oven for 2$^{1}/_{2}$ hours.

4 Remove the casserole from the oven, add the ham and olives and return it to the oven to cook for a further 30 minutes, or until the beef is very tender. Discard the orange rind and serve straight from the casserole, garnished with parsley sprigs.

beef goulash

ingredients

SERVES 4

2 tbsp vegetable oil

1 large onion, chopped

1 garlic clove, crushed

750 g/1 lb 10 oz lean stewing
    steak, cut into chunks

2 tbsp paprika

425 g/15 oz canned chopped
    tomatoes

2 tbsp tomato purée

1 large red pepper, deseeded
    and chopped

175 g/6 oz mushrooms, sliced

600 ml/1 pint beef stock

1 tbsp cornflour

1 tbsp water

salt and pepper

chopped fresh parsley,
    to garnish

freshly cooked long-grain and
    wild rice, to serve

method

1 Heat the oil in a large frying pan and cook the onion and garlic for 3–4 minutes.

2 Add the stewing steak and cook over a high heat for 3 minutes, until browned all over. Add the paprika and stir well, then add the tomatoes, tomato purée, red pepper and mushrooms. Cook for 2 minutes, stirring frequently.

3 Pour in the beef stock. Bring to the boil, then reduce the heat. Cover and simmer for 1 1/2–2 hours, until the meat is tender.

4 Blend the cornflour with the water, then add to the pan, stirring until thickened and smooth. Cook for 1 minute, then season to taste with salt and pepper.

5 Transfer the beef goulash to a warmed serving dish, garnish with chopped fresh parsley and serve with rice.

chilli con carne

ingredients

SERVES 4

750 g/1 lb 10 oz lean stewing
   steak
2 tbsp vegetable oil
1 large onion, sliced
2–4 garlic cloves, crushed
1 tbsp plain flour
425 ml/15 fl oz tomato juice
400 g/14 oz canned chopped
   tomatoes
1–2 tbsp sweet chilli sauce
1 tsp ground cumin
425 g/15 oz canned red
   kidney beans, drained
   and rinsed
1/2 tsp dried oregano
1–2 tbsp chopped fresh
   parsley, plus extra sprigs
   to garnish
salt and pepper
freshly cooked rice and
   tortillas, to serve

method

1 Preheat the oven to 160°C/325°F/Gas Mark 3. Using a sharp knife, cut the beef into 2-cm/ 3/4-inch cubes. Heat the oil in a large flameproof casserole dish and fry the beef over a medium heat until well sealed on all sides. Remove the beef from the casserole with a slotted spoon and reserve until required.

2 Add the onion and garlic to the casserole and fry until lightly browned; then stir in the flour and cook for 1–2 minutes.

3 Stir in the tomato juice and tomatoes and bring to the boil. Return the beef to the casserole and add the chilli sauce, cumin and salt and pepper to taste. Cover and cook in the preheated oven for 11/2 hours, or until the beef is almost tender.

4 Stir in the kidney beans, oregano and chopped parsley, and adjust the seasoning to taste, if necessary. Cover the casserole and return to the oven for 45 minutes. Transfer to 4 large warmed serving plates, garnish with parsley sprigs and serve immediately with freshly cooked rice and tortillas.

beef stroganoff

ingredients

SERVES 4

15 g/^{1}/$_2$ oz dried ceps

350 g/12 oz beef fillet

2 tbsp olive oil

115 g/4 oz shallots, sliced

175 g/6 oz chestnut
    mushrooms

^{1}/$_2$ tsp Dijon mustard

5 tbsp double cream

salt and pepper

freshly cooked pasta, to serve

fresh chives, to garnish

method

1 Place the dried ceps in a bowl and cover with hot water. Leave to soak for 20 minutes. Meanwhile, cut the beef against the grain into 5 mm/^{1}/$_4$ inch thick slices, then into 1 cm/ ^{1}/$_2$ inch long strips, and reserve.

2 Drain the mushrooms, reserving the soaking liquid, and chop. Strain the soaking liquid through a fine-mesh sieve or coffee filter and reserve.

3 Heat half the oil in a large frying pan. Add the shallots and cook over a low heat, stirring occasionally, for 5 minutes, or until softened. Add the soaked mushrooms, reserved soaking water and whole chestnut mushrooms and cook, stirring frequently, for 10 minutes, or until almost all of the liquid has evaporated, then transfer the mixture to a plate.

4 Heat the remaining oil in the frying pan, add the beef and cook, stirring frequently, for 4 minutes, or until browned all over. You may need to do this in batches. Return the mushroom mixture to the frying pan and season to taste with salt and pepper.

5 Place the mustard and cream in a small bowl and stir to mix, then fold into the meat and mushroom mixture. Heat through gently, then serve with freshly cooked pasta and garnish with chives.

beef & vegetable stew with sweetcorn

ingredients

SERVES 4

450 g/1 lb braising steak

1 1/2 tbsp plain flour

1 tsp hot paprika

1–1 1/2 tsp chilli powder

1 tsp ground ginger

2 tbsp olive oil

1 large onion, cut into chunks

3 garlic cloves, sliced

2 celery sticks, sliced

225 g/8 oz carrots, chopped

300 ml/10 fl oz lager

300 ml/10 fl oz beef stock

350 g/12 oz potatoes, chopped

1 red pepper, deseeded and
    chopped

2 corn on the cob, halved

115 g/4 oz tomatoes,
    quartered

115 g/4 oz shelled fresh or
    frozen peas

1 tbsp chopped fresh
    coriander

salt and pepper

method

1 Trim any fat or gristle from the beef and cut into 2.5-cm/1-inch chunks. Mix the flour and spices together. Toss the beef in the spiced flour until well coated.

2 Heat the oil in a large heavy-based saucepan and cook the onion, garlic and celery, stirring frequently, for 5 minutes, or until softened. Add the beef and cook over a high heat, stirring frequently, for 3 minutes, or until browned on all sides and sealed.

3 Add the carrots, then remove from the heat. Gradually stir in the lager and stock, then return to the heat and bring to the boil, stirring. Reduce the heat, cover and simmer, stirring occasionally, for 1 1/2 hours.

4 Add the potatoes to the saucepan and simmer for a further 15 minutes. Add the red pepper and corn on the cob and simmer for a further 15 minutes, then add the tomatoes and peas and simmer for a further 10 minutes, or until the beef and vegetables are tender. Season to taste with salt and pepper, stir in the coriander and serve.

beef pepper pot stew

ingredients

450 g/1 lb braising steak

1^1/$_2$ tbsp plain flour

2 tbsp olive oil

1 Spanish onion, chopped

3–4 garlic cloves, crushed

1 fresh green chilli, deseeded
    and chopped

3 celery sticks, sliced

4 whole cloves

1 tsp ground allspice

1–2 teaspoons hot pepper
    sauce, or to taste

600 ml/1 pint beef stock

225 g/8 oz deseeded and
    peeled squash, such
    as acorn, cut into small
    chunks

1 large red pepper, deseeded
    and chopped

4 tomatoes, roughly chopped

115 g/4 oz okra, trimmed and
    halved

freshly cooked mixed wild and
    basmati rice, to serve

method

1 Trim any fat or gristle from the beef and cut into 2.5-cm/1-inch chunks. Toss the beef in the flour until well coated and reserve any remaining flour.

2 Heat the oil in a large heavy-based saucepan and cook the onion, garlic, chilli and celery with the cloves and allspice, stirring frequently, for 5 minutes, or until softened. Add the beef and cook over a high heat, stirring frequently, for 3 minutes, or until browned on all sides and sealed. Sprinkle in the reserved flour and cook, stirring constantly, for 2 minutes, then remove from the heat.

3 Add the hot pepper sauce and gradually stir in the stock, then return to the heat and bring to the boil, stirring. Reduce the heat, cover and simmer, stirring occasionally, for 1^1/$_2$ hours.

4 Add the squash and red pepper to the saucepan and simmer for a further 15 minutes. Add the tomatoes and okra and simmer for a further 15 minutes, or until the beef is tender. Serve with cooked mixed wild and basmati rice.

beef chop suey

ingredients

SERVES 4

450 g/1 lb ribeye or sirloin
   steak, thinly sliced
2 tbsp vegetable or groundnut
   oil
1 onion, thinly sliced
2 sticks celery, thinly sliced
   diagonally
1 head of broccoli, cut into
   small florets, blanched
225 g/8 oz mangetout, sliced
   in half lengthways
55 g/2 oz canned bamboo
   shoots, rinsed and
   julienned
8 water chestnuts, thinly
   sliced
225 g/8 oz mushrooms, thinly
   sliced
1 tbsp oyster sauce
1 tsp salt

marinade

1 tbsp Shaoxing rice wine
pinch of white pepper
pinch of salt
1 tbsp light soy sauce
$1/2$ tsp sesame oil

method

1 Combine all the marinade ingredients in a bowl and marinate the beef for at least 20 minutes.

2 In a preheated wok or deep pan, heat 1 tablespoon of the oil and stir-fry the beef until the colour has changed. Remove and set aside. Wipe out the wok or pan with kitchen paper.

3 In the clean wok or deep pan, heat the remaining oil and stir-fry the onion for 1 minute. Add the celery and broccoli and cook for 2 minutes. Add the mangetout, bamboo shoots, water chestnuts and mushrooms and cook for 1 minute. Add the beef, season with the oyster sauce and salt and serve.

caramelized lamb shanks

ingredients

SERVES 4

4 tbsp clear honey

1 tbsp vegetable oil

1 tsp dried thyme or oregano

2 tsp pepper

$1/2$ tsp salt

4 lamb shanks, about
    400 g/14 oz each

350–500 ml/12–18 fl oz stock

1 head garlic, unpeeled, sliced
    in half across the centre

1 onion, quartered

1 parsnip, quartered
    lengthways

4 small salad potatoes, halved
    lengthways

4 small carrots

method

1 Preheat the oven to 180°C/ 350°F/Gas Mark 4. Mix together the honey, oil, thyme, pepper and salt, and rub all over the lamb shanks. Place the lamb shanks in a roasting tin with 200 ml/7 fl oz of the stock, the garlic and onion.

2 Cook in the preheated oven for 1 hour, turning the lamb after 30 minutes. Turn again, and add the parsnip, potatoes, carrots and 150 ml/5 fl oz of the remaining stock. Cook for a further 30 minutes and turn the lamb again. Add a little more stock, if necessary, then cook for a further 15 minutes.

3 Using a slotted spoon, transfer the meat and vegetables to a warmed serving dish. Using kitchen paper, remove any excess fat from the surface of the liquid in the tin. Place the tin over a medium heat and stir for a few seconds, until the liquid is syrupy. Pour over the meat and vegetables, and serve immediately.

slow-cooked lamb with celeriac

ingredients

SERVES 4

1 leg of lamb, on the bone, weighing 2.5 kg/5 lb 8 oz

2 whole heads garlic

grated rind of 2 lemons and juice of 1

2 tbsp finely chopped fresh rosemary

3 tbsp extra virgin olive oil

3 shallots, roughly chopped

350 ml/12 fl oz dry white wine

1 kg/2 lb 4 oz celeriac, peeled and cut into large chunks

salt and pepper

method

1 Score gently through the fat on the lamb in a diamond pattern. Put in a non-metallic dish. Separate the heads of garlic into cloves. Peel and crush 4 of the garlic cloves and reserve the remainder. Mix the crushed garlic, lemon rind and juice and rosemary together. Season well with salt and pepper and stir in the oil. Rub the mixture all over the meat. Cover and marinate in the refrigerator for several hours, or overnight.

2 Preheat the oven to 220°C/425°F/Gas Mark 7. Transfer the lamb to a roasting tin and pour over the marinade. Roast in the preheated oven for 20 minutes.

3 Reduce the oven temperature to 190°C/ 375°F/Gas Mark 5. Add the reserved whole garlic cloves, shallots and wine, cover with foil and roast for a further 1 hour 40 minutes, basting occasionally. Remove the foil, add the celeriac and turn to coat in the pan juices. Cook with the lamb for a further 20 minutes.

4 Remove from the oven, lift out the lamb and keep warm. Return the celeriac to the oven and roast for a further 10–15 minutes, until golden.

5 Carve the lamb and serve with the celeriac and whole garlic cloves, drizzling over the pan juices.

irish stew

ingredients

SERVES 4

4 tbsp plain flour

1.3 kg/3 lb middle neck
   of lamb, trimmed of
   visible fat

3 large onions, chopped

3 carrots, sliced

450 g/1 lb potatoes,
   quartered

$1/2$ tsp dried thyme

850 ml/$1^{1}/2$ pints beef stock

salt and pepper

2 tbsp chopped fresh parsley,
   to garnish

method

1 Preheat the oven to 160°C/325°F/Gas Mark 3. Spread the flour on a plate and season to taste with salt and pepper. Roll the pieces of lamb in the flour to coat, shaking off any excess, and arrange in the base of a casserole.

2 Layer the onions, carrots and potatoes on top of the lamb.

3 Sprinkle in the thyme and pour in the stock, then cover and cook in the preheated oven for $2^{1}/2$ hours. Garnish with the chopped fresh parsley and serve straight from the casserole.

lamb stew with chickpeas

ingredients

SERVES 4–6

6 tbsp olive oil

225 g/8 oz chorizo sausage,
cut into 5 mm/1/4 inch
thick slices, casings
removed

2 large onions, chopped

6 large garlic cloves, crushed

900 g/2 lb boned leg of lamb,
cut into 5-cm/2-inch
chunks

250 ml/9 fl oz lamb stock
or water

125 ml/4 fl oz red wine, such
as Rioja or Tempranillo

2 tbsp sherry vinegar

800 g/1 lb 12 oz canned
chopped tomatoes

4 fresh thyme sprigs, plus
extra to garnish

2 bay leaves

1/2 tsp sweet Spanish paprika

800 g/1 lb 12 oz canned
chickpeas, rinsed and
drained

salt and pepper

method

1 Preheat the oven to 160°C/325°F/Gas Mark 3. Heat 4 tablespoons of the oil in a large heavy-based flameproof casserole over a medium–high heat. Reduce the heat, add the chorizo and fry for 1 minute; set aside. Add the onions to the casserole and fry for 2 minutes, then add the garlic and continue frying for 3 minutes, or until the onions are soft but not brown. Remove from the casserole and set aside.

2 Heat the remaining 2 tablespoons of oil in the casserole. Add the lamb cubes in a single layer without over-crowding the casserole, and fry until browned on each side; work in batches, if necessary.

3 Return the onion mixture to the casserole with all the lamb. Stir in the stock, wine, vinegar, tomatoes with their juices and salt and pepper to taste. Bring to the boil, scraping any glazed bits from the base of the casserole. Reduce the heat and stir in the thyme, bay leaves and paprika.

4 Transfer to the preheated oven and cook, covered, for 40–45 minutes, until the lamb is tender. Stir in the chickpeas and return to the oven, uncovered, for 10 minutes, or until they are heated through and the juices are reduced.

5 Taste and adjust the seasoning. Serve garnished with thyme sprigs.

mediterranean lamb with apricots & pistachio nuts

ingredients

SERVES 4

pinch of saffron threads

2 tbsp almost-boiling water

450 g/1 lb lean boneless
    lamb, such as leg steaks

1^1/$_2$ tbsp plain flour

1 tsp ground coriander

^{1}/$_2$ tsp ground cumin

^{1}/$_2$ tsp ground allspice

1 tbsp olive oil

1 onion, chopped

2–3 garlic cloves, chopped

450 ml/16 fl oz lamb or
    chicken stock

1 cinnamon stick, bruised

85 g/3 oz dried apricots,
    roughly chopped

175 g/6 oz courgettes, sliced

115 g/4 oz cherry tomatoes

1 tbsp chopped fresh
    coriander

salt and pepper

2 tbsp roughly chopped
    pistachio nuts, to garnish

freshly cooked couscous,
    to serve

method

1 Put the saffron threads in a heatproof jug with the water and leave for at least 10 minutes to infuse. Trim off any fat or gristle from the lamb and cut into 2.5-cm/1-inch chunks. Mix the flour and spices together, then toss the lamb in the spiced flour until well coated and reserve any remaining spiced flour.

2 Heat the oil in a large heavy-based saucepan and cook the onion and garlic, stirring frequently, for 5 minutes, or until softened. Add the lamb and cook over a high heat, stirring frequently, for 3 minutes, or until browned on all sides and sealed. Sprinkle in the reserved spiced flour and cook, stirring constantly, for
2 minutes, then remove from the heat.

3 Gradually stir in the stock and the saffron with its soaking liquid, then return to the heat and bring to the boil, stirring. Add the cinnamon stick and apricots. Reduce the heat, cover and simmer, stirring occasionally, for 1 hour.

4 Add the courgettes and tomatoes and cook for a further 15 minutes. Discard the cinnamon stick. Stir in the fresh coriander and season to taste with salt and pepper. Sprinkle with the pistachio nuts and serve with couscous.

country lamb casserole

ingredients

SERVES 6

2 tbsp sunflower oil

2 kg/4 lb 8 oz boneless leg of
    lamb, cut into 2.5-cm/
    1-inch cubes

6 leeks, sliced

1 tbsp plain flour

150 ml/5 fl oz rosé wine

300 ml/10 fl oz chicken stock

1 tbsp tomato purée

1 tbsp sugar

2 tbsp chopped fresh mint,
    plus extra sprigs to garnish

115 g/4 oz dried apricots,
    chopped

1 kg/2 lb 4 oz potatoes, sliced

3 tbsp melted unsalted butter

salt and pepper

method

1 Preheat the oven to 180°C/350°F/Gas Mark 4. Heat the oil in a large flameproof casserole. Add the lamb in batches and cook over a medium heat, stirring, for 5–8 minutes, or until browned. Transfer to a plate.

2 Add the leeks to the casserole and cook, stirring occasionally, for 5 minutes, or until softened. Sprinkle in the flour and cook, stirring, for 1 minute. Pour in the wine and stock and bring to the boil, stirring. Stir in the tomato purée, sugar, chopped mint and apricots and season to taste with salt and pepper.

3 Return the lamb to the casserole and stir. Arrange the potato slices on top and brush with the melted butter. Cover and bake in the preheated oven for 1$1/2$ hours.

4 Increase the oven temperature to 200°C/400°F/Gas Mark 6, uncover the casserole and bake for a further 30 minutes, or until the potato topping is golden brown. Serve immediately, garnished with mint sprigs.

azerbaijani lamb pilau

ingredients

SERVES 4

2–3 tbsp vegetable oil

650 g/1 lb 7 oz boneless
    lamb shoulder, cut into
    2.5-cm/1-inch cubes

2 onions, roughly chopped

1 tsp ground cumin

200 g/7 oz arborio rice

1 tbsp tomato purée

1 tsp saffron threads

100 ml/3 fl oz pomegranate
    juice

850 ml/1 1/2 pints lamb stock,
    chicken stock or water

115 g/4 oz ready-to-eat dried
    apricots or prunes, halved

2 tbsp raisins

salt and pepper

shredded fresh mint and
    watercress, to serve

method

1 Heat the oil in a large flameproof casserole or saucepan over a high heat. Add the lamb, in batches, and cook over a high heat, turning frequently, for 7 minutes, or until lightly browned.

2 Add the onions, reduce the heat to medium and cook for 2 minutes, or until beginning to soften. Add the cumin and rice and cook, stirring to coat, for 2 minutes, or until the rice is translucent. Stir in the tomato purée and the saffron threads.

3 Add the pomegranate juice and stock. Bring to the boil, stirring. Stir in the apricots and raisins. Reduce the heat to low, cover, and simmer for 20–25 minutes, or until the lamb and rice are tender and all of the liquid has been absorbed.

4 Season to taste with salt and pepper, then sprinkle the shredded mint and watercress over the pilau and serve straight from the casserole.

pot-roast pork

ingredients

SERVES 4

1 tbsp sunflower oil

55 g/2 oz butter

1 kg/2 lb 4 oz boned and
    rolled pork loin joint

4 shallots, chopped

6 juniper berries

2 fresh thyme sprigs, plus
    extra to garnish

150 ml/5 fl oz dry cider

150 ml/5 fl oz chicken stock
    or water

8 celery sticks, chopped

2 tbsp plain flour

150 ml/5 fl oz double cream

salt and pepper

freshly cooked peas, to serve

method

1 Heat the oil with half the butter in a heavy-based saucepan or flameproof casserole. Add the pork and cook over a medium heat, turning frequently, for 5–10 minutes, or until browned. Transfer to a plate.

2 Add the shallots to the saucepan and cook, stirring frequently, for 5 minutes, or until softened. Add the juniper berries and thyme sprigs and return the pork to the saucepan, with any juices that have collected on the plate. Pour in the cider and stock, season to taste with salt and pepper, then cover and simmer for 30 minutes. Turn the pork over and add the celery. Re-cover the pan and cook for a further 40 minutes.

3 Meanwhile, make a beurre manié by mashing the remaining butter with the flour in a small bowl. Transfer the pork and celery to a platter with a slotted spoon and keep warm. Remove and discard the juniper berries and thyme. Whisk the beurre manié, a little at a time, into the simmering cooking liquid. Cook, stirring constantly, for 2 minutes, then stir in the cream and bring to the boil.

4 Slice the pork and spoon a little of the sauce over it. Garnish with thyme sprigs and serve immediately with the celery, peas and the remaining sauce.

pork & vegetable stew

ingredients

SERVES 4

450 g/1 lb lean boneless pork
1¹/₂ tbsp plain flour
1 tsp ground coriander
1 tsp ground cumin
1¹/₂ tsp ground cinnamon
1 tbsp olive oil
1 onion, chopped
400 g/14 oz canned chopped
   tomatoes
2 tbsp tomato purée
300–450 ml/10–16 fl oz
   chicken stock
225 g/8 oz carrots, chopped
350 g/12 oz squash, such
   as kabocha, peeled,
   deseeded and chopped
225 g/8 oz leeks, sliced,
   blanched and drained
115 g/4 oz okra, trimmed
   and sliced
salt and pepper
fresh parsley sprigs, to garnish
freshly cooked couscous,
   to serve

method

1 Trim off any fat or gristle from the pork and cut into thin strips about 5 cm/2 inches long. Mix the flour and spices together. Toss the pork in the spiced flour until well coated and reserve any remaining spiced flour.

2 Heat the oil in a large heavy-based saucepan and cook the onion, stirring frequently, for 5 minutes, or until softened. Add the pork and cook over a high heat, stirring frequently, for 5 minutes, or until browned on all sides and sealed. Sprinkle in the reserved spiced flour and cook, stirring constantly, for 2 minutes, then remove from the heat.

3 Gradually stir the tomatoes to the saucepan. Blend the tomato purée with a little of the stock in a jug and gradually stir into the saucepan, then stir in half the remaining stock.

4 Add the carrots, then return to the heat and bring to the boil, stirring. Reduce the heat, cover and simmer, stirring occasionally, for 1¹/₂ hours. Add the squash and cook for a further 15 minutes.

5 Add the leeks and okra, and the remaining stock if you prefer a thinner sauce. Simmer for a further 15 minutes, or until the pork and vegetables are tender. Season to taste with salt and pepper, then garnish with parsley sprigs and serve with couscous.

sausage & bean casserole

ingredients

SERVES 4

8 Italian sausages

3 tbsp olive oil

1 large onion, chopped

2 garlic cloves, chopped

1 green pepper, deseeded
and sliced

225g/8 oz fresh tomatoes,
skinned and chopped
or 400 g/14 oz canned
chopped tomatoes

2 tbsp sun-dried tomato paste

400 g/14 oz canned
cannellini beans, drained

mashed potatoes, to serve

method

1 Prick the sausages all over with a fork. Heat 2 tablespoons of the oil in a large heavy-based frying pan. Add the sausages and cook over a low heat, turning frequently, for 10–15 minutes, until evenly browned and cooked through. Remove them from the frying pan and keep warm. Drain off the oil and wipe out the pan with kitchen paper.

2 Heat the remaining oil in the frying pan. Add the onion, garlic and green pepper to the frying pan and cook for 5 minutes, stirring occasionally, or until softened.

3 Add the tomatoes to the frying pan and leave the mixture to simmer for about 5 minutes, stirring occasionally, or until slightly reduced and thickened.

4 Stir the sun-dried tomato paste, cannellini beans and sausages into the mixture in the frying pan. Cook for 4–5 minutes, or until the mixture is piping hot. Add 4–5 tablespoons of water if the mixture becomes too dry during cooking.

5 Transfer to serving plates and serve with mashed potatoes.

oriental pork

ingredients

SERVES 4

450 g/1 lb lean boneless pork

1¹/₂ tbsp plain flour

1–2 tbsp olive oil

1 onion, cut into small
    wedges

2–3 garlic cloves, chopped

2.5-cm/1-inch piece fresh
    ginger, peeled and grated

1 tbsp tomato purée

300 ml/10 fl oz chicken stock

225 g/8 oz canned pineapple
    chunks in natural juice

1–1¹/₂ tbsp dark soy sauce

1 red pepper, deseeded and
    sliced

1 green pepper, deseeded
    and sliced

1¹/₂ tbsp balsamic vinegar

4 spring onions, diagonally
    sliced, to garnish

method

1 Trim off any fat or gristle from the pork and cut into 2.5-cm/1-inch chunks. Toss the pork in the flour until well coated and reserve any remaining flour.

2 Heat the oil in a large heavy-based saucepan and cook the onion, garlic and ginger, stirring frequently, for 5 minutes, or until softened. Add the pork and cook over a high heat, stirring frequently, for 5 minutes, or until browned on all sides and sealed. Sprinkle in the reserved flour and cook, stirring constantly, for 2 minutes, then remove from the heat.

3 Blend the tomato purée with the stock in a heatproof jug and gradually stir into the saucepan. Drain the pineapple, reserving both the fruit and juice, and stir the juice into the saucepan.

4 Add the soy sauce to the saucepan, then return to the heat and bring to the boil, stirring. Reduce the heat, cover and simmer, stirring occasionally, for 1 hour. Add the peppers and cook for a further 15 minutes, or until the pork is tender. Stir in the vinegar and the reserved pineapple and heat through for 5 minutes. Serve sprinkled with the spring onions.

red curry pork with peppers

ingredients

SERVES 4

2 tbsp vegetable or groundnut
oil

1 onion, roughly chopped

2 garlic cloves, chopped

450 g/1 lb pork fillet, thickly
sliced

1 red pepper, deseeded and
cut into squares

175 g/6 oz mushrooms,
quartered

2 tbsp Thai red curry paste

115 g/4 oz creamed coconut,
chopped

300 ml/10 fl oz pork stock or
vegetable stock

2 tbsp Thai soy sauce

4 tomatoes, peeled, deseeded
and chopped

handful of fresh coriander,
chopped

freshly cooked noodles,
to serve

method

1 Heat the oil in a wok or large frying pan and fry the onion and garlic for 1–2 minutes, until they are softened but not browned.

2 Add the pork and stir-fry for 2–3 minutes, until browned all over. Add the red pepper, mushrooms and curry paste.

3 Dissolve the coconut in the stock and add to the wok with the soy sauce. Bring to the boil and simmer for 4–5 minutes, until the liquid has reduced and thickened.

4 Add the tomatoes and coriander and cook for 1–2 minutes before serving with noodles.

poultry

Poultry, particularly chicken, is extremely versatile and goes well with a wide range of other ingredients and flavours. It's also suited to all kinds of one-pot cooking – from stews and casseroles to roasts and risottos. It can be cooked whole, cut into quarters or smaller pieces on the bone, or boned and diced. As almost everyone likes it, chicken is a great choice for family meals.

Combining chicken with different herbs, spices and other flavourings gives each dish individuality, so there's no risk of getting bored. A Middle Eastern stew of diced chicken breast, vegetables, chickpeas and apricots, lightly spiced with cumin and cinnamon, couldn't be more different from a whole bird roasted with potatoes, peppers and courgettes, for example. It is just as good cooked in red or white wine as it is with chillies, ginger and coconut milk.

Turkey and duck recipes add variety and a hint of something special to the menu, making these dishes ideal for informal entertaining. As both turkey and duck have a tendency to dry out during cooking, one-pot recipes incorporating a richly flavoured sauce will ensure success. Fillets, steaks and duck legs are inexpensive so you'll find they'll easily fit your family budget whilst adding variety to your culinary repertoire.

chicken & barley stew

ingredients

SERVES 4

2 tbsp vegetable oil

8 small skinless chicken thighs

500 ml/18 fl oz chicken stock

100 g/3^1/$_2$ oz pearl barley,
rinsed and drained

200 g/7 oz small new
potatoes, scrubbed and
halved lengthways

2 large carrots, peeled
and sliced

1 leek, trimmed and sliced

2 shallots, sliced

1 tbsp tomato purée

1 bay leaf

1 courgette, trimmed and
sliced

2 tbsp chopped fresh flat-leaf
parsley, plus extra sprigs
to garnish

2 tbsp plain flour

salt and pepper

fresh crusty bread, to serve

method

1 Heat the oil in a large saucepan over a medium heat. Add the chicken and cook for 3 minutes, then turn over and cook on the other side for a further 2 minutes. Add the stock, pearl barley, potatoes, carrots, leek, shallots, tomato purée and bay leaf. Bring to the boil, lower the heat and simmer for 30 minutes.

2 Add the courgette and chopped parsley, cover the pan and cook for a further 20 minutes, or until the chicken is cooked through. Remove the bay leaf and discard.

3 In a separate bowl, mix the flour with 4 tablespoons of water to make a smooth paste. Add it to the stew and cook, stirring, over a low heat for a further 5 minutes. Season to taste with salt and pepper.

4 Remove from the heat, ladle into individual serving bowls and garnish with parsley sprigs. Serve with fresh crusty bread.

coq au vin

ingredients

SERVES 4

55 g/2 oz butter

2 tbsp olive oil

1.8 kg/4 lb chicken pieces

115 g/4 oz rindless smoked
    bacon, cut into strips

115 g/4 oz baby onions

115 g/4 oz chestnut
    mushrooms, halved

2 garlic cloves, finely chopped

2 tbsp brandy

225 ml/8 fl oz red wine

300 ml/10 fl oz chicken stock

1 bouquet garni

2 tbsp plain flour

salt and pepper

bay leaves, to garnish

method

1 Melt half the butter with the oil in a large flameproof casserole. Add the chicken and cook over a medium heat, stirring, for 8–10 minutes, or until golden brown all over. Add the bacon, onions, mushrooms and garlic.

2 Pour in the brandy and set it alight with a match or taper. When the flames have died down, add the wine, stock and bouquet garni and season to taste with salt and pepper. Bring to the boil, reduce the heat and simmer gently for 1 hour, or until the chicken pieces are cooked through and tender.

3 Meanwhile, make a beurre manié by mashing the remaining butter with the flour in a small bowl.

4 Remove and discard the bouquet garni from the casserole. Transfer the chicken to a large plate and keep warm. Stir the beurre manié into the casserole, a little at a time. Bring to the boil, then return the chicken to the casserole to warm through. Serve, garnished with bay leaves.

all-in-one roast chicken

ingredients

SERVES 6

2.5 kg/5 lb 8 oz chicken

fresh rosemary sprigs

175 g/6 oz feta cheese,
    coarsely grated

2 tbsp sun-dried tomato paste

55 g/2 oz butter, softened

1 bulb garlic, broken into
    cloves but not peeled

1 kg/2 lb 4 oz new potatoes,
    halved if large

1 each red, green and yellow
    pepper, deseeded and
    cut into chunks

3 courgettes, thinly sliced

2 tbsp olive oil

2 tbsp plain flour

600 ml/1 pint chicken stock

salt and pepper

method

1 Preheat the oven to 190°C/375°F/Gas Mark 5. Rinse the chicken with cold water and drain well. Carefully cut between the skin and the top of the breast meat. Slide a finger into the slit and carefully enlarge it to form a pocket. Continue until the skin is completely lifted away from both breasts and the top of the legs.

2 Chop the leaves from 3 rosemary stems. Mix with the feta cheese, sun-dried tomato paste, butter and pepper to taste, then spoon under the skin. Put the chicken in a large roasting tin, cover with foil and cook in the preheated oven for 40 minutes.

3 Remove the roasting tin from the oven and add the garlic and vegetables to the chicken. Drizzle with the oil, tuck in a few rosemary sprigs and season to taste with salt and pepper.

4 Cook for a further 40 minutes, then remove the foil. Return to the oven and cook for a further 40 minutes, until the chicken is browned and the juices run clear when a skewer is inserted into the thickest part of the meat.

5 Transfer the chicken and vegetables to a serving platter. Spoon the fat out of the roasting tin and stir the flour into the remaining cooking juices. Place the roasting tin on top of the hob and cook over a medium heat for 2 minutes, then gradually stir in the stock. Bring to the boil, stirring until thickened. Serve with the chicken and vegetables.

spicy aromatic chicken

ingredients

SERVES 4

4–8 chicken pieces, skinned

1/2 lemon, cut into wedges

4 tbsp olive oil

1 onion, roughly chopped

2 large garlic cloves, finely
    chopped

125 ml/4 fl oz dry white wine

400 g/14 oz canned chopped
    tomatoes

pinch of sugar

1/2 tsp ground cinnamon

1/2 tsp ground cloves

1/2 tsp ground allspice

400 g/14 oz canned artichoke
    hearts or okra, drained

8 black olives, stoned

salt and pepper

method

1 Rub the chicken pieces with the lemon. Heat the oil in a large flameproof casserole or lidded frying pan. Add the onion and garlic and fry for 5 minutes, until softened. Add the chicken pieces and fry for 5–10 minutes, until browned on all sides.

2 Pour in the wine and add the tomatoes with their juice, the sugar, cinnamon, cloves, allspice and salt and pepper to taste and bring to the boil. Cover the casserole and simmer for 45 minutes–1 hour, until the chicken is tender.

3 Meanwhile, if using artichoke hearts, cut them in half. Add the artichokes or okra and the olives to the casserole 10 minutes before the end of cooking, and continue to simmer until heated through. Serve hot.

brunswick stew

ingredients

SERVES 6

1.8 kg/4 lb chicken pieces

2 tbsp paprika

2 tbsp olive oil

25 g/1 oz butter

450 g/1 lb onions, chopped

2 yellow peppers, deseeded
and chopped

400 g/14 oz canned chopped
tomatoes

225 ml/8 fl oz dry white wine

450 ml/16 fl oz chicken stock

1 tbsp Worcestershire sauce

$^1/_2$ tsp Tabasco sauce

1 tbsp finely chopped fresh
parsley, plus extra
to garnish

325 g/11$^1/_2$ oz canned
sweetcorn kernels,
drained

425 g/15 oz canned butter
beans, drained and rinsed

2 tbsp plain flour

4 tbsp water

salt

method

1 Season the chicken pieces with salt to taste and dust with paprika.

2 Heat the oil and butter in a flameproof casserole or large saucepan. Add the chicken pieces and cook over a medium heat, turning, for 10–15 minutes, or until golden. Transfer to a plate with a slotted spoon.

3 Add the onions and peppers to the casserole. Cook over a low heat, stirring occasionally, for 5 minutes, or until softened. Add the tomatoes, wine, stock, Worcestershire sauce, Tabasco sauce and chopped parsley and bring to the boil, stirring. Return the chicken to the casserole, cover and simmer, stirring occasionally, for 30 minutes.

4 Add the sweetcorn and beans to the casserole, partially re-cover and simmer for a further 30 minutes. Place the flour and water in a small bowl and mix to make a paste. Stir a ladleful of the cooking liquid into the paste, then stir it into the stew. Cook, stirring frequently, for 5 minutes. Serve, garnished with parsley.

chicken in white wine

ingredients

SERVES 4

55 g/2 oz butter

2 tbsp olive oil

2 rindless, thick streaky
   bacon rashers, chopped

115 g/4 oz baby onions,
   peeled

1 garlic clove, finely chopped

1.8 kg/4 lb chicken pieces

400 ml/14 fl oz dry white wine

300 ml/10 fl oz chicken stock

1 bouquet garni

115 g/4 oz button mushrooms

25 g/1 oz plain flour

salt and pepper

fresh herb sprigs, to garnish

method

1 Preheat the oven to 160°C/325°F/Gas Mark 3. Melt half the butter with the oil in a flameproof casserole. Add the bacon and cook over a medium heat, stirring, for 5–10 minutes, or until golden brown. Transfer the bacon to a large plate. Add the onions and garlic to the casserole and cook over a low heat, stirring occasionally, for 10 minutes, or until golden. Transfer to the plate. Add the chicken and cook over a medium heat, stirring constantly, for 8–10 minutes, or until golden. Transfer to the plate.

2 Drain off any excess fat from the casserole. Stir in the wine and stock and bring to the boil, scraping any sediment off the base. Add the bouquet garni and season to taste with salt and pepper. Return the bacon, onions, garlic and chicken to the casserole. Cover and cook in the preheated oven for 1 hour.

3 Add the mushrooms, re-cover and cook for 15 minutes. Meanwhile, make a beurre manié by mashing the remaining butter with the flour in a small bowl.

4 Remove the casserole from the oven and set over a medium heat. Discard the bouquet garni. Whisk in the beurre manié, a little at a time. Bring to the boil, stirring constantly, then serve, garnished with fresh herb sprigs.

florida chicken

ingredients

SERVES 4

450 g/1 lb skinless, boneless chicken

1½ tbsp plain flour

1 tbsp olive oil

1 onion, cut into wedges

2 celery sticks, sliced

150 ml/5 fl oz orange juice

300 ml/10 fl oz chicken stock

1 tbsp light soy sauce

1–2 tsp clear honey

1 tbsp grated orange rind

1 orange pepper, deseeded and chopped

225 g/8 oz courgettes, sliced into half moons

2 small corn on the cob, halved, or 100 g/3½ oz baby corn

1 orange, peeled and segmented

salt and pepper

1 tbsp chopped fresh parsley, to garnish

method

1 Lightly rinse the chicken and pat dry with kitchen paper. Cut into bite-sized pieces. Season the flour well with salt and pepper. Toss the chicken in the seasoned flour until well coated and reserve any remaining seasoned flour.

2 Heat the oil in a large heavy-based frying pan and cook the chicken over a high heat, stirring frequently, for 5 minutes, or until golden on all sides and sealed. Using a slotted spoon, transfer the chicken to a plate.

3 Add the onion and celery to the frying pan and cook over a medium heat, stirring frequently, for 5 minutes, or until softened. Sprinkle in the reserved seasoned flour and cook, stirring constantly, for 2 minutes, then remove from the heat. Gradually stir in the orange juice, stock, soy sauce and honey, followed by the orange rind, then return to the heat and bring to the boil, stirring.

4 Return the chicken to the frying pan. Reduce the heat, cover and simmer, stirring occasionally, for 15 minutes. Add the orange pepper, courgettes and corn on the cob and simmer for a further 10 minutes, or until the chicken and vegetables are tender. Add the orange segments, stir well and heat through for 1 minute. Serve garnished with the parsley.

thai green chicken curry

ingredients

SERVES 4

2 tbsp groundnut oil

500 g/1 lb 2 oz skinless,
    boneless chicken breasts,
    cut into cubes

2 kaffir lime leaves, roughly torn

1 lemon grass stalk, finely
    chopped

225 ml/8 fl oz canned
    coconut milk

16 baby aubergines, halved

2 tbsp Thai fish sauce

fresh Thai basil sprigs and
    shredded kaffir lime
    leaves, to garnish

green curry paste

16 fresh green chillies

2 shallots, sliced

4 kaffir lime leaves

1 lemon grass stalk, chopped

2 garlic cloves, chopped

1 tsp cumin seeds

1 tsp coriander seeds

1 tbsp grated fresh ginger
    or galangal

1 tsp grated lime rind

5 black peppercorns

1 tbsp sugar

2 tbsp groundnut oil

method

1 First make the curry paste. Deseed the chillies, if you like, and roughly chop. Place all the paste ingredients except the oil in a mortar and pound with a pestle. Alternatively, process in a food processor. Gradually blend in the oil. Set aside.

2 Heat a wok or large heavy-based frying pan and add the oil. When the oil is hot, add 2 tablespoons of the curry paste and stir-fry briefly until all the aromas are released.

3 Add the chicken, lime leaves and lemon grass and stir-fry for 3–4 minutes, until the meat is beginning to colour. Add the coconut milk and aubergines and simmer gently for 8–10 minutes, or until tender.

4 Stir in the fish sauce and serve immediately, garnished with Thai basil sprigs and shredded lime leaves.

chicken tagine

ingredients

SERVES 4

1 tbsp olive oil
1 onion, cut into small
    wedges
2–4 garlic cloves, sliced
450 g/1 lb skinless, boneless
    chicken breast, diced
1 tsp ground cumin
2 cinnamon sticks, lightly
    bruised
1 tbsp plain wholemeal flour
225 g/8 oz aubergine, diced
1 red pepper, deseeded and
    chopped
85 g/3 oz button mushrooms,
    sliced
1 tbsp tomato purée
600 ml/1 pint chicken stock
280 g/10 oz canned
    chickpeas, drained and
    rinsed
55 g/2 oz ready-to-eat dried
    apricots, chopped
salt and pepper
1 tbsp chopped fresh
    coriander, to garnish

method

1 Heat the oil in a large saucepan over a medium heat, add the onion and garlic and cook for 3 minutes, stirring frequently. Add the chicken and cook, stirring constantly, for a further 5 minutes, or until sealed on all sides. Add the cumin and cinnamon sticks to the saucepan halfway through sealing the chicken.

2 Sprinkle in the flour and cook, stirring constantly, for 2 minutes.

3 Add the aubergine, red pepper and mushrooms and cook for a further 2 minutes, stirring constantly.

4 Blend the tomato purée with the stock, stir into the saucepan and bring to the boil. Reduce the heat and add the chickpeas and apricots. Cover and simmer for 15–20 minutes, or until the chicken is tender.

5 Season to taste with salt and pepper and serve immediately, sprinkled with coriander.

mexican chicken, chilli & potato pot

Ingredients

SERVES 4

2 tbsp vegetable oil

450 g/1 lb boneless, skinless
  chicken breasts, cubed

1 onion, finely chopped

1 green pepper, deseeded
  and finely chopped

1 potato, diced

1 sweet potato, diced

2 garlic cloves, very finely
  chopped

1–2 fresh green chillies,
  deseeded and finely
  chopped

200 g/7 oz canned chopped
  tomatoes

1/2 tsp dried oregano

1/2 tsp salt

4 tsp pepper

4 tbsp chopped fresh
  coriander

450 ml/16 fl oz chicken stock

method

1 Heat the oil in a large heavy-based saucepan over a medium–high heat. Cook the chicken until lightly browned.

2 Reduce the heat to medium. Add the onion, green pepper, potato and sweet potato. Cover and cook for 5 minutes, stirring occasionally, until the vegetables begin to soften.

3 Add the garlic and chillies. Cook for 1 minute. Stir in the tomatoes, oregano, salt, pepper and half the coriander. Cook for 1 minute.

4 Pour in the stock. Bring to the boil, then cover and simmer over a low–medium heat for 15–20 minutes, or until the chicken is cooked through and the vegetables are tender.

5 Sprinkle with the remaining coriander just before serving.

chicken jalfrezi

ingredients

SERVES 4

$1/2$ tsp cumin seeds

$1/2$ tsp coriander seeds

1 tsp mustard oil

3 tbsp vegetable oil

1 large onion, finely chopped

3 garlic cloves, crushed

1 tbsp tomato purée

2 tomatoes, peeled and
    chopped

1 tsp ground turmeric

$1/2$ tsp chilli powder

$1/2$ tsp garam masala

1 tsp red wine vinegar

1 small red pepper, deseeded
    and chopped

125 g/$4^1/2$ oz frozen broad
    beans

500 g/1 lb 2 oz cooked
    chicken, chopped

salt

fresh coriander sprigs,
    to garnish

freshly cooked rice, to serve

method

1 Grind the cumin and coriander seeds in a mortar with a pestle, then reserve. Heat the mustard oil in a large heavy-based frying pan over a high heat for 1 minute, or until it begins to smoke. Add the vegetable oil, reduce the heat and add the onion and garlic. Cook for 10 minutes, or until golden.

2 Add the tomato purée, tomatoes, turmeric, ground cumin and coriander seeds, chilli powder, garam masala and vinegar to the frying pan. Stir the mixture until fragrant.

3 Add the red pepper and broad beans and stir for a further 2 minutes, or until the pepper is softened. Stir in the chicken, and season to taste with salt. Simmer gently for 6–8 minutes, or until the chicken is heated through and the beans are tender.

4 Transfer to warmed serving bowls, garnish with coriander sprigs and serve with freshly cooked rice.

balti chicken

ingredients

SERVES 6

3 tbsp ghee or vegetable oil

2 large onions, sliced

3 tomatoes, sliced

1/2 tsp kalonji seeds

4 black peppercorns

2 cardamom pods

1 cinnamon stick

1 tsp chilli powder

1 tsp garam masala

1 tsp garlic paste

1 tsp ginger paste

700 g/1 lb 9 oz skinless,
   boneless chicken breasts
   or thighs, diced

2 tbsp natural yogurt

2 tbsp chopped fresh
   coriander, plus extra
   sprigs to garnish

2 fresh green chillies,
   deseeded and finely
   chopped

2 tbsp lime juice

salt

method

1 Heat the ghee in a large heavy-based frying pan. Add the onions and cook over a low heat, stirring occasionally, for 10 minutes, or until golden. Add the tomatoes, kalonji seeds, peppercorns, cardamom pods, cinnamon stick, chilli powder, garam masala, garlic paste and ginger paste, and season to taste with salt. Cook, stirring constantly, for 5 minutes.

2 Add the chicken and cook, stirring constantly, for 5 minutes, or until well coated in the spice paste. Stir in the yogurt. Cover and simmer, stirring occasionally, for 10 minutes.

3 Stir in the chopped coriander, chillies and lime juice. Transfer to a warmed serving dish, garnish with coriander sprigs and serve immediately.

louisiana chicken

ingredients

SERVES 4

5 tbsp sunflower oil

4 chicken portions

55 g/2 oz plain flour

1 onion, chopped

2 celery sticks, sliced

1 green pepper, deseeded
   and chopped

2 garlic cloves, finely chopped

2 tsp chopped fresh thyme,
   plus extra to garnish

2 fresh red chillies, deseeded
   and finely chopped

400 g/14 oz canned chopped
   tomatoes

300 ml/10 fl oz chicken stock

salt and pepper

method

1 Heat the oil in a heavy-based saucepan or flameproof casserole. Add the chicken and cook over a medium heat, stirring, for 5–10 minutes, or until golden. Transfer the chicken to a plate with a slotted spoon.

2 Stir the flour into the oil and cook over a very low heat, stirring constantly, for 15 minutes, or until golden. Do not let it burn. Immediately add the onion, celery and green pepper and cook, stirring constantly, for 2 minutes. Add the garlic, thyme and chillies and cook, stirring, for 1 minute.

3 Stir in the tomatoes and their juices, then gradually stir in the stock. Return the chicken pieces to the saucepan, cover and simmer for 45 minutes, or until the chicken is cooked through and tender. Season to taste with salt and pepper, transfer to warmed serving plates and serve immediately, garnished with a sprinkling of chopped thyme.

chicken pepperonata

ingredients

SERVES 4

8 skinless chicken thighs
2 tbsp wholemeal flour
2 tbsp olive oil
1 small onion, thinly sliced
1 garlic clove, crushed
1 each large red, yellow and
    green peppers, deseeded
    and thinly sliced
400 g/14 oz canned chopped
    tomatoes
1 tbsp chopped oregano, plus
    extra to garnish
salt and pepper
crusty wholemeal bread,
    to serve

method

1 Toss the chicken thighs in the flour, shaking off the excess.

2 Heat the oil in a wide frying pan and fry the chicken quickly until sealed and lightly browned, then remove from the pan.

3 Add the onion to the pan and gently fry until soft. Add the garlic, peppers, tomatoes and oregano, then bring to the boil, stirring.

4 Arrange the chicken over the vegetables, season well with salt and pepper, then cover the pan tightly and simmer for 20–25 minutes, or until the chicken is completely cooked and tender.

5 Taste and adjust the seasoning if necessary, garnish with oregano and serve with crusty wholemeal bread.

chicken risotto with saffron

ingredients

SERVES 4

125 g/4^1/$_2$ oz butter

900 g/2 lb skinless, boneless
  chicken breasts, thinly
  sliced

1 large onion, chopped

500 g/1 lb 2 oz risotto rice

150 ml/5 fl oz white wine

1 tsp crumbled saffron
  threads

1.3 litres/2^1/$_4$ pints chicken
  stock

55 g/2 oz freshly grated
  Parmesan cheese

salt and pepper

method

1 Heat 55 g/2 oz of the butter in a deep saucepan. Add the chicken and onion and cook, stirring frequently, for 8 minutes, or until golden brown.

2 Add the rice and mix to coat in the butter. Cook, stirring constantly for 2–3 minutes, or until the grains are translucent. Add the wine and cook, stirring constantly, for 1 minute, until reduced.

3 Mix the saffron with 4 tablespoons of the hot stock. Add the liquid to the rice and cook, stirring constantly, until it is absorbed.

4 Gradually add the remaining hot stock, a ladle at a time. Stir constantly and add more liquid as the rice absorbs each addition. Cook for 20 minutes, or until all the liquid is absorbed and the rice is creamy. Season to taste with salt and pepper.

5 Remove the risotto from the heat and add the remaining butter. Mix well, then stir in the Parmesan until it melts. Spoon the risotto onto warmed plates and serve immediately.

mexican turkey

ingredients

SERVES 4

55 g/2 oz plain flour

4 turkey breast fillets

3 tbsp sunflower oil

1 onion, thinly sliced

1 red pepper, deseeded and
    sliced

300 ml/10 fl oz chicken stock

25 g/1 oz raisins

4 tomatoes, peeled, deseeded
    and chopped

1 tsp chilli powder

$1/2$ tsp ground cinnamon

pinch of ground cumin

25 g/1 oz plain chocolate,
    finely chopped or grated

salt and pepper

fresh coriander sprigs,
    to garnish

method

1 Preheat the oven to 160°C/325°F/Gas Mark 3. Spread the flour on a plate and season to taste with salt and pepper. Coat the turkey fillets in the seasoned flour, shaking off any excess. Reserve the seasoned flour.

2 Heat the oil in a flameproof casserole. Add the turkey fillets and cook over a medium heat, turning occasionally, for 5–10 minutes, or until golden. Transfer to a plate with a slotted spoon.

3 Add the onion and red pepper to the casserole. Cook over a low heat, stirring occasionally, for 5 minutes, or until softened. Sprinkle in any remaining seasoned flour and cook, stirring constantly, for 1 minute.

4 Gradually stir in the stock, then add the raisins, tomatoes, chilli powder, cinnamon, cumin and chocolate. Season to taste with salt and pepper. Bring to the boil, stirring constantly.

5 Return the turkey to the casserole, cover and cook in the preheated oven for 50 minutes. Serve immediately, garnished with coriander sprigs.

italian turkey steaks

ingredients

SERVES 4

1 tbsp olive oil

4 turkey escalopes or steaks

2 red peppers, deseeded
    and sliced

1 red onion, sliced

2 garlic cloves, finely chopped

300 ml/10 fl oz passata

150 ml/5 fl oz medium white
    wine

1 tbsp chopped fresh
    marjoram

400 g/14 oz canned
    cannellini beans, drained
    and rinsed

3 tbsp fresh white
    breadcrumbs

salt and pepper

fresh basil sprigs, to garnish

method

1 Heat the oil in a flameproof casserole or heavy-based frying pan. Add the turkey escalopes and cook over a medium heat for 5–10 minutes, turning occasionally, until golden. Transfer to a plate.

2 Add the red pepper and onion to the casserole and cook over a low heat, stirring occasionally, for 5 minutes, or until softened. Add the garlic and cook for a further 2 minutes.

3 Return the turkey to the casserole and add the passata, wine and marjoram. Season to taste with salt and pepper. Bring to the boil, then reduce the heat, cover and simmer, stirring occasionally, for 25–30 minutes, or until the turkey is cooked through and tender.

4 Preheat the grill to medium. Stir the cannellini beans into the casserole and simmer for a further 5 minutes. Sprinkle the breadcrumbs over the top and place under the preheated grill for 2–3 minutes, or until golden. Serve, garnished with fresh basil sprigs.

duck legs with olives

ingredients

SERVES 4

4 duck legs, all visible fat
    trimmed off
800 g/1 lb 12 oz canned
    chopped tomatoes
8 garlic cloves, peeled, but
    left whole
1 large onion, finely chopped
1 carrot, peeled and finely
    chopped
1 celery stick, peeled and
    finely chopped
3 fresh thyme sprigs
100 g/3^1/$_2$ oz Spanish green
    olives in brine, stuffed
    with pimientos, garlic or
    almonds, drained and
    rinsed
1 tsp finely grated orange rind
salt and pepper

method

1 Put the duck legs in the base of a flameproof casserole or a large heavy-based frying pan with a tight-fitting lid. Add the tomatoes, garlic, onion, carrot, celery, thyme and olives and stir together. Season to taste with salt and pepper.

2 Turn the heat to high and cook, uncovered, until the ingredients begin to bubble. Reduce the heat to low, cover tightly and simmer for 1^1/$_4$–1^1/$_2$ hours, until the duck is very tender. Check occasionally and add a little water if the mixture appears to be drying out.

3 When the duck is tender, transfer it to a serving platter, cover and keep hot. Leave the casserole uncovered, increase the heat to medium and cook, stirring, for about 10 minutes, until the mixture forms a sauce. Stir in the orange rind, then taste and adjust the seasoning if necessary.

4 Mash the tender garlic cloves with a fork and spread over the duck legs. Spoon the sauce over the top. Serve at once.

duck jambalaya-style stew

ingredients

SERVES 4

4 duck breasts, about 150 g/
 5^1/$_2$ oz each
2 tbsp olive oil
225 g/8 oz gammon, cut into
 small chunks
225 g/8 oz chorizo, outer
 casing removed
1 onion, chopped
3 garlic cloves, chopped
3 celery sticks, chopped
1–2 fresh red chillies,
 deseeded and chopped
1 green pepper, deseeded
 and chopped
600 ml/1 pint chicken stock
1 tbsp chopped fresh oregano
400 g/14 oz canned chopped
 tomatoes
1–2 tsp hot pepper sauce,
 or to taste
chopped fresh flat-leaf
 parsley, to garnish
green salad and freshly
 cooked rice, to serve

method

1 Remove and discard the skin and any fat from the duck breasts. Cut the flesh into bite-sized pieces.

2 Heat half the oil in a large deep frying pan and cook the duck, gammon and chorizo over a high heat, stirring frequently, for 5 minutes, or until browned on all sides and sealed. Using a slotted spoon, remove from the frying pan and set aside.

3 Add the onion, garlic, celery and chillies to the frying pan and cook over a medium heat, stirring frequently, for 5 minutes, or until softened. Add the green pepper, then stir in the stock, oregano, tomatoes and hot pepper sauce.

4 Bring to the boil, then reduce the heat and return the duck, gammon and chorizo to the frying pan. Cover and simmer, stirring occasionally, for 20 minutes, or until the duck and gammon are tender.

5 Serve immediately, garnished with parsley and accompanied by a green salad and rice.

fish & seafood

Virtually every country with a coastline boasts its own fish and seafood speciality and, more often than not, this will be a one-pot dish. Yet they are all distinctive, whether a hot Indian biryani with succulent prawns nestling in golden fluffy rice, a colourful Spanish stew of mixed fish and shellfish or a subtly spiced Moroccan tagine redolent with the fragrances of lemon and coriander. Cooks worldwide have all reached the same conclusion – that where fish is concerned, more is often best. In this context, more implies a wealth of complementary ingredients cooked with the fish or, very frequently, a medley of fish and seafood.

As well as stews, curries and risottos, one-pot fish dishes may be roasted, griddled, poached or baked in parcels. Roasted fish and seafood are a sensational taste revelation and certainly special enough to serve to guests, while parcels are both easy to prepare and fun to serve. Besides this range of cooking techniques, there is also a great choice of fish and seafood with different flavours, textures and colours. Nutritionists recommend that we should eat fish at least twice a week and, with this choice of delicious, easy and varied one-pot dishes, that couldn't be easier.

spanish seafood stew

ingredients

SERVES 4–6

large pinch of saffron threads

4 tbsp almost-boiling water

6 tbsp olive oil

1 large onion, chopped

2 garlic cloves, finely chopped

1^1/$_2$ tbsp chopped fresh
thyme leaves

2 bay leaves

2 red peppers, deseeded and
roughly chopped

800 g/1 lb 12 oz canned
chopped tomatoes

1 tsp smoked paprika

250 ml/9 fl oz fish stock

140 g/5 oz blanched
almonds, toasted and
finely ground

12–16 live mussels, scrubbed
and debearded

12–16 live clams, scrubbed

600 g/1 lb 5 oz thick boneless
hake or cod fillets, skinned
and cut into 5-cm/2-inch
chunks

12–16 raw prawns, peeled
and deveined

salt and pepper

thick crusty bread, to serve

method

1 Put the saffron in a jug with the water and infuse for at least 10 minutes.

2 Heat the oil in a large heavy-based flameproof casserole over a medium–high heat. Reduce the heat to low and cook the onion, stirring occasionally, for 10 minutes, or until golden but not browned. Stir in the garlic, thyme, bay leaves and peppers and cook, stirring frequently, for 5 minutes, or until the peppers are softened and the onions have softened further.

3 Add the tomatoes and paprika and simmer, stirring frequently, for a further 5 minutes.

4 Stir in the stock, saffron and its soaking liquid and the almonds and bring to the boil, stirring. Reduce the heat and simmer for 5–10 minutes, until the sauce reduces. Season to taste with salt and pepper.

5 Meanwhile, discard any mussels and clams with broken shells and any that refuse to close when tapped.

6 Gently stir the fish into the stew, then add the prawns, mussels and clams. Reduce the heat to very low, cover and simmer for 5 minutes, or until the fish is opaque, the mussels and clams have opened and the prawns have turned pink. Discard any mussels or clams that remain closed. Serve immediately with crusty bread.

squid with parsley & pine kernels

ingredients

SERVES 4

85 g/3 oz sultanas

5 tbsp olive oil

6 tbsp chopped fresh flat-leaf
  parsley, plus extra
  to garnish

2 garlic cloves, finely chopped

800 g/1 lb 12 oz prepared
  squid, sliced, or squid rings

125 ml/4 fl oz dry white wine

500 g/1 lb 2 oz passata

pinch of chilli powder

85 g/3 oz pine kernels, finely
  chopped

salt

method

1 Place the sultanas in a small bowl, cover with lukewarm water and set aside for 15 minutes to plump up.

2 Meanwhile, heat the oil in a heavy-based saucepan. Add the parsley and garlic and cook over a low heat, stirring frequently, for 3 minutes. Add the squid and cook, stirring occasionally, for 5 minutes.

3 Increase the heat to medium, pour in the wine and cook until it has almost completely evaporated. Stir in the passata and season to taste with chilli powder and salt. Lower the heat again, cover and simmer gently, stirring occasionally, for 45–50 minutes, until the squid is almost tender.

4 Drain the sultanas and stir them into the saucepan with the pine kernels. Let simmer for a further 10 minutes, then serve immediately garnished with chopped parsley.

seafood in saffron sauce

ingredients

SERVES 4

225 g/8 oz live mussels

225 g/8 oz live clams

2 tbsp olive oil

1 onion, sliced

pinch of saffron threads

1 tbsp chopped fresh thyme

2 garlic cloves, finely chopped

800 g/1 lb 12 oz canned
   tomatoes, drained and
   chopped

175 ml/6 fl oz dry white wine

2 litres/3$\frac{1}{2}$ pints fish stock

350 g/12 oz red mullet fillets,
   cut into bite-sized chunks

450 g/1 lb monkfish fillets,
   cut into bite-sized chunks

225 g/8 oz raw squid rings

2 tbsp fresh shredded basil
   leaves

salt and pepper

fresh crusty bread, to serve

method

1 Clean the mussels and clams by scrubbing or scraping the shells and pulling out any beards that are attached to the mussels. Discard any with broken shells and any that refuse to close when tapped.

2 Heat the oil in a large flameproof casserole and cook the onion with the saffron, thyme and a pinch of salt over a low heat, stirring occasionally, for 5 minutes, or until softened. Add the garlic and cook, stirring, for 2 minutes.

3 Add the tomatoes, wine and stock, season to taste with salt and pepper and stir well. Bring to the boil, then reduce the heat and simmer for 15 minutes.

4 Add the fish chunks and simmer for a further 3 minutes. Add the clams, mussels and squid rings and simmer for a further 5 minutes, or until the mussels and clams have opened. Discard any that remain closed. Stir in the basil and serve immediately, accompanied by plenty of fresh crusty bread to mop up the broth.

seafood hotpot with red wine & tomatoes

ingredients

SERVES 4–6

350 g/12 oz mussels, scrubbed and debearded

4 tbsp olive oil

1 onion, finely chopped

1 green pepper, deseeded and chopped

2 garlic cloves, very finely chopped

5 tbsp tomato purée

1 tbsp chopped fresh flat-leaf parsley

1 tsp dried oregano

400 g/14 oz canned chopped tomatoes

225 ml/8 fl oz dry red wine

450 g/1 lb firm white fish, such as cod or monkfish, cut into 5-cm/2-inch pieces

115 g/4 oz scallops, halved

115 g/4 oz raw prawns, shelled and deveined

200 g/7 oz canned crabmeat

salt and pepper

10–15 fresh basil leaves, shredded, to garnish

method

1 Discard any mussels with broken shells and any that refuse to close when tapped.

2 Heat the oil in a heavy-based saucepan or flameproof casserole over a medium heat. Add the onion and green pepper and cook for 5 minutes, or until beginning to soften.

3 Stir in the garlic, tomato purée, parsley and oregano and cook for 1 minute, stirring.

4 Pour in the tomatoes and wine. Season to taste with salt and pepper.

5 Bring to the boil, then cover and simmer over a low heat for 30 minutes. Add the fish, cover and simmer for 15 minutes.

6 Add the mussels, scallops, prawns and crabmeat. Cover and cook for a further 15 minutes. Discard any mussels that remain closed. Stir in the basil just before serving.

moroccan fish tagine

ingredients

SERVES 4

2 tbsp olive oil

1 large onion, finely chopped

pinch of saffron threads

$1/2$ tsp ground cinnamon

1 tsp ground coriander

$1/2$ tsp ground cumin

$1/2$ tsp ground turmeric

200 g/7 oz canned chopped
tomatoes

300 ml/10 fl oz fish stock

4 small red mullet, cleaned,
boned and heads and tails
removed

55 g/2 oz stoned green olives

1 tbsp chopped preserved
lemon

3 tbsp chopped fresh coriander

salt and pepper

freshly cooked couscous,
to serve

method

1 Heat the oil in a flameproof casserole. Add the onion and cook gently over a very low heat, stirring occasionally, for 10 minutes, or until softened but not coloured. Add the saffron, cinnamon, ground coriander, cumin and turmeric and cook for a further 30 seconds, stirring constantly.

2 Add the tomatoes and stock and stir well. Bring to the boil, reduce the heat, cover and simmer for 15 minutes. Uncover and simmer for 20–35 minutes, or until thickened.

3 Cut each red mullet in half, then add the fish pieces to the casserole, pushing them down into the liquid. Simmer the stew for a further 5–6 minutes, or until the fish is just cooked.

4 Carefully stir in the olives, preserved lemon and chopped coriander. Season to taste with salt and pepper and serve immediately with couscous.

seafood chilli

ingredients

SERVES 4

115 g/4 oz raw prawns,
   peeled and deveined
250 g/9 oz prepared scallops,
   thawed if frozen
115 g/4 oz monkfish fillet,
   cut into chunks
1 lime, peeled and thinly
   sliced
1 tbsp chilli powder
1 tsp ground cumin
3 tbsp chopped fresh
   coriander
2 garlic cloves, finely chopped
1 fresh green chilli, deseeded
   and chopped
3 tbsp sunflower oil
1 onion, roughly chopped
1 red pepper, deseeded and
   roughly chopped
1 yellow pepper, deseeded
   and roughly chopped
1/4 tsp ground cloves
pinch of ground cinnamon
pinch of cayenne pepper
350 ml/12 fl oz fish stock
400 g/14 oz canned chopped
   tomatoes
400 g/14 oz canned red
   kidney beans, drained
   and rinsed
salt

method

1 Place the prawns, scallops, monkfish and lime in a large non-metallic dish with 1/4 teaspoon of the chilli powder, 1/4 teaspoon of the ground cumin, 1 tablespoon of the chopped coriander, half the garlic, the fresh chilli and 1 tablespoon of the oil. Cover with clingfilm and leave to marinate for up to 1 hour.

2 Meanwhile, heat 1 tablespoon of the remaining oil in a flameproof casserole or large heavy-based saucepan. Add the onion, the remaining garlic and the red and yellow peppers and cook over a low heat, stirring occasionally, for 5 minutes, or until softened.

3 Add the remaining chilli powder, the remaining cumin, the cloves, cinnamon and cayenne pepper with the remaining oil, if necessary, and season to taste with salt. Cook, stirring,
for 5 minutes, then gradually stir in the stock and the tomatoes and their juices. Partially cover and simmer for 25 minutes.

4 Add the beans to the tomato mixture and spoon the fish and shellfish on top. Cover and cook for 10 minutes, or until the fish and shellfish are cooked through. Sprinkle with the remaining coriander and serve.

mediterranean fish stew

ingredients

SERVES 4

2 tbsp olive oil

1 onion, sliced

pinch of saffron threads,
    lightly crushed

1 tbsp chopped fresh thyme

2 garlic cloves, finely chopped

800 g/1 lb 12 oz canned
    chopped tomatoes,
    drained

2 litres/3¹/₂ pints fish stock

175 ml/6 fl oz dry white wine

350 g/12 oz red mullet fillets,
    cut into chunks

450 g/1 lb monkfish fillets,
    cut into chunks

450 g/1 lb fresh clams,
    scrubbed

225 g/8 oz squid rings

2 tbsp fresh basil leaves,
    plus extra to garnish

salt and pepper

method

1 Heat the oil in a large flameproof casserole. Add the onion, saffron, thyme and a pinch of salt. Cook over a low heat, stirring occasionally, for 5 minutes, or until the onion has softened.

2 Add the garlic and cook for a further 2 minutes, then add the drained tomatoes and pour in the stock and wine. Season to taste with salt and pepper, bring the mixture to the boil, then reduce the heat and simmer for 15 minutes.

3 Add the chunks of mullet and monkfish and simmer for 3 minutes.

4 Discard any clams with broken shells and any that refuse to close when tapped. Add the remaining clams and squid to the casserole and simmer for 5 minutes, or until the clam shells have opened.

5 Discard any clams that remain closed. Tear the basil leaves and stir into the stew. Serve garnished with basil leaves.

italian fish stew

ingredients

SERVES 4

2 tbsp olive oil

2 red onions, finely chopped

1 garlic clove, crushed

2 courgettes, sliced

400 g/14 oz canned chopped
   tomatoes

850 ml/1^1/$_2$ pints fish or
   vegetable stock

85 g/3 oz dried pasta shapes

350 g/12 oz firm white fish,
   such as cod, haddock
   or hake

1 tbsp chopped fresh basil or
   oregano, plus extra
   to garnish

1 tsp grated lemon rind

1 tbsp cornflour

1 tbsp water

salt and pepper

method

1 Heat the oil in a large pan. Add the onions and garlic and cook over a low heat, stirring occasionally, for about 5 minutes, until softened. Add the courgettes and cook, stirring frequently, for 2–3 minutes.

2 Add the tomatoes and stock to the pan and bring to the boil. Add the pasta, bring back to the boil, reduce the heat and cover. Simmer for 5 minutes.

3 Skin and bone the fish, then cut it into chunks. Add to the pan with the basil and lemon rind and simmer gently for 5 minutes, until the fish is opaque and flakes easily (take care not to overcook it) and the pasta is tender, but still firm to the bite.

4 Place the cornflour and water in a small bowl, mix to a smooth paste and stir into the stew. Cook gently for 2 minutes, stirring constantly, until thickened. Season to taste with salt and pepper.

5 Ladle the stew into 4 warmed soup bowls. Garnish with basil and serve immediately.

moules marinières

ingredients

SERVES 4

2 kg/4 lb 8 oz live mussels

300 ml/10 fl oz dry white wine

6 shallots, finely chopped

1 bouquet garni

pepper

4 bay leaves, to garnish

fresh crusty bread, to serve

method

1 Clean the mussels by scrubbing or scraping the shells and pulling off any beards. Discard any with broken shells and any that refuse to close when tapped with a knife. Rinse the mussels under cold running water.

2 Pour the wine into a large heavy-based saucepan, add the shallots and bouquet garni and season to taste with pepper. Bring to the boil over a medium heat. Add the mussels, cover tightly and cook, shaking the saucepan occasionally, for 5 minutes.

3 Remove and discard the bouquet garni and any mussels that remain closed. Divide the mussels among 4 soup plates with a slotted spoon. Tilt the casserole to let any sand settle, then spoon the cooking liquid over the mussels. Garnish with bay leaves and serve immediately with fresh crusty bread.

goan-style seafood curry

ingredients

SERVES 4–6

3 tbsp vegetable or
  groundnut oil
1 tbsp black mustard seeds
12 fresh or 1 tbsp dried curry
  leaves
6 shallots, finely chopped
1 garlic clove, crushed
1 tsp ground turmeric
$1/2$ tsp ground coriander
$1/4$–$1/2$ tsp chilli powder
140 g/5 oz creamed coconut,
  grated and dissolved in
  300 ml/10 fl oz boiling
  water
500 g/1 lb 2 oz skinless,
  boneless white fish, such
  as monkfish or cod, cut
  into large chunks
450 g/1 lb large raw prawns,
  peeled and deveined
finely grated rind and juice
  of 1 lime
salt
lime wedges, to serve

method

1 Heat the oil in a wok or large frying pan over a high heat. Add the mustard seeds and stir them around for about 1 minute, or until they jump. Stir in the curry leaves.

2 Add the shallots and garlic and stir for about 5 minutes, or until the shallots are golden. Stir in the turmeric, ground coriander and chilli powder and continue stirring for about 30 seconds.

3 Add the dissolved creamed coconut. Bring to the boil, then reduce the heat to medium and stir for about 2 minutes.

4 Reduce the heat to low, add the fish and simmer for 1 minute, spooning the sauce over the fish and very gently stirring it around. Add the prawns and continue to simmer for a further 4–5 minutes, until the fish flesh flakes easily and the prawns turn pink and curl.

5 Add half the lime juice, then taste and add more lime juice and salt to taste. Sprinkle with the lime rind and serve with lime wedges.

jambalaya

ingredients

SERVES 4

2 tbsp vegetable oil

2 onions, roughly chopped

1 green pepper, deseeded
   and roughly chopped

2 celery sticks, roughly
   chopped

3 garlic cloves, finely chopped

2 tsp paprika

300 g/10^1/$_2$ oz skinless,
   boneless chicken breasts,
   chopped

100 g/3^1/$_2$ oz kabanos
   sausages, chopped

3 tomatoes, peeled and
   chopped

450 g/1 lb long-grain rice

850 ml/1^1/$_2$ pints hot chicken
   or fish stock

1 tsp dried oregano

2 bay leaves

12 large raw prawns, peeled
   and deveined

4 spring onions, finely chopped

2 tbsp chopped fresh parsley,
   plus extra to garnish

salt and pepper

method

1 Heat the oil in a large frying pan over a low heat. Add the onions, green pepper, celery and garlic and cook for 8–10 minutes, until all the vegetables have softened. Add the paprika and cook for a further 30 seconds.

2 Add the chicken and sausages and cook for 8–10 minutes, until lightly browned. Add the tomatoes and cook for 2–3 minutes, until they have collapsed.

3 Add the rice to the pan and stir well. Pour in the stock, oregano and bay leaves and stir well. Cover and simmer for 10 minutes.

4 Add the prawns and stir. Cover again and cook for a further 6–8 minutes, until the rice is tender and the prawns are cooked through.

5 Stir in the spring onions and parsley and season to taste with salt and pepper. Transfer to a large serving dish, garnish with chopped parsley and serve.

prawns with coconut rice

ingredients

SERVES 4

115 g/4 oz dried Chinese
 mushrooms
1 tbsp vegetable or
 groundnut oil
6 spring onions, chopped
55 g/2 oz desiccated coconut
1 fresh green chilli, deseeded
 and chopped
225 g/8 oz jasmine rice
150 ml/5 fl oz fish stock
400 ml/14 fl oz coconut milk
350 g/12 oz cooked peeled
 prawns
6 fresh Thai basil sprigs

method

1 Place the mushrooms in a small bowl, cover with hot water and set aside to soak for 30 minutes. Drain, then cut off and discard the stalks and slice the caps.

2 Heat the oil in a wok and stir-fry the spring onions, coconut and chilli for 2–3 minutes, until lightly browned. Add the mushrooms and stir-fry for 3–4 minutes.

3 Add the rice and stir-fry for 2–3 minutes, then add the stock and bring to the boil. Lower the heat and add the coconut milk. Simmer for 10–15 minutes, until the rice is tender. Stir in the prawns and basil, heat through and serve.

prawn biryani

ingredients

SERVES 8

1 tsp saffron threads

50 ml/2 fl oz tepid water

2 shallots, roughly chopped

3 garlic cloves, crushed

1 tsp chopped fresh ginger

2 tsp coriander seeds

$^1/_2$ tsp black peppercorns

2 cloves

seeds from 2 green
   cardamom pods

2.5-cm/1-inch piece
   cinnamon stick

1 tsp ground turmeric

1 fresh green chilli, chopped

$^1/_2$ tsp salt

2 tbsp ghee

1 tsp black mustard seeds

400 g/14 oz raw tiger prawns,
   peeled and deveined

300 ml/10 fl oz coconut milk

300 ml/10 fl oz low-fat natural
   yogurt

freshly cooked basmati rice,
   to serve

to garnish

flaked almonds, toasted

1 spring onion, sliced

fresh coriander sprigs

method

1 Soak the saffron in the tepid water for 10 minutes. Put the shallots, garlic, ginger, dry spices, chilli and salt into a spice grinder or mortar and grind to a paste.

2 Heat the ghee in a saucepan and add the mustard seeds. When they start to pop, add the prawns and stir over a high heat for 1 minute. Stir in the spice mix, then the coconut milk and yogurt. Simmer for 20 minutes.

3 Spoon the prawn mixture into serving bowls. Top with the freshly cooked basmati rice and drizzle over the saffron water. Serve garnished with the flaked almonds, spring onion slices and coriander sprigs.

prawn & chicken paella

ingredients

SERVES 6–8

16 live mussels, scrubbed
and debearded

$1/2$ tsp saffron threads

2 tbsp hot water

350 g/12 oz medium-grain
paella rice

6 tbsp olive oil

6–8 unboned chicken thighs,
skin-on but with excess fat
removed

140 g/5 oz Spanish chorizo
sausage, casing removed,
cut into 5-mm/ $1/4$-inch
slices

2 large onions, chopped

4 large garlic cloves, crushed

1 tsp mild or hot Spanish
paprika, to taste

100 g/$3^{1}/2$ oz green beans,
chopped

125 g/$4^{1}/2$ oz frozen peas

1.3 litres/$2^{1}/4$ pints fish stock,
chicken stock or vegetable
stock

16 raw prawns, peeled and
deveined

2 red peppers, halved and
deseeded, then grilled,
peeled and sliced

salt and pepper

35 g/$1^{1}/4$ oz fresh chopped
parsley, to garnish

method

1 Discard any mussels with broken shells and any that refuse to close when tapped. Put the saffron and hot water in a bowl and infuse for a few minutes. Meanwhile, put the rice in a sieve and rinse until the water runs clear. Set aside.

2 Heat half the oil in a paella pan or ovenproof casserole. Cook the chicken over medium–high heat, turning frequently, for 5 minutes, or until golden. Transfer to a bowl. Add the chorizo to the pan and cook, stirring, for 1 minute, or until beginning to crisp. Add to the chicken.

3 Heat the remaining oil in the pan and cook the onions, stirring frequently, for 2 minutes, then add the garlic and paprika and cook for a further 3 minutes.

4 Add the drained rice, beans and peas and stir until coated in oil. Return the chicken and chorizo and any juices to the pan. Stir in the stock, saffron and its soaking liquid, and salt and pepper to taste and bring to the boil, stirring constantly. Reduce the heat to low and let simmer, uncovered and without stirring, for 15 minutes, or until the rice is almost tender.

5 Arrange the mussels, prawns and red peppers on top, then cover and simmer, without stirring, until the prawns turn pink and the mussels open. Discard any mussels that remain closed. Sprinkle with parsley and serve.

seafood risotto

ingredients

SERVES 4

1 tbsp olive oil

55 g/2 oz butter

2 garlic cloves, chopped

350 g/12 oz risotto rice

1.3 litres/2$\frac{1}{4}$ pints fish stock
  or chicken stock

250 g/9 oz mixed cooked
  seafood, such as prawns,
  squid, mussels and clams

2 tbsp chopped fresh
  oregano, plus extra
  to garnish

55 g/2 oz freshly grated
  pecorino or Parmesan
  cheese

salt and pepper

method

1 Heat the oil with 25 g/1 oz of the butter in a deep saucepan over a medium heat until the butter has melted. Add the garlic and cook, stirring, for 1 minute.

2 Reduce the heat, add the rice and mix to coat in oil and butter. Cook, stirring constantly, for 2–3 minutes, or until the grains are translucent.

3 Gradually add the hot stock, a ladle at a time. Stir constantly and add more liquid as the rice absorbs each addition. Increase the heat to medium so that the liquid bubbles. Cook for 20 minutes, or until all the liquid is absorbed and the rice is creamy.

4 About 5 minutes before the rice is ready, add the seafood and oregano to the saucepan and mix well.

5 Remove the saucepan from the heat and season to taste with salt and pepper. Add the remaining butter and mix well, then stir in the grated cheese until it melts. Spoon onto warmed plates and serve immediately, garnished with oregano.

swordfish with tomatoes & olives

ingredients

SERVES 4

2 tbsp olive oil

1 onion, finely chopped

1 celery stick, finely chopped

115 g/4 oz green olives, stoned

450 g/1 lb tomatoes, chopped

3 tbsp bottled capers, drained

4 swordfish steaks, about
    140 g/5 oz each

salt and pepper

fresh flat-leaf parsley sprigs,
    to garnish

method

1 Heat the oil in a large heavy-based frying pan. Add the onion and celery and cook over a low heat, stirring occasionally, for 5 minutes, or until softened.

2 Meanwhile, roughly chop half the olives. Add the chopped and whole olives to the pan with the tomatoes and capers, stir, and season to taste with salt and pepper.

3 Bring to the boil, then reduce the heat, cover and simmer gently, stirring occasionally, for 15 minutes.

4 Add the swordfish steaks to the frying pan and return to the boil. Cover and simmer for 20 minutes, or until the fish is cooked and the flesh flakes easily, turning the fish once during cooking. Transfer the fish to serving plates and spoon over the sauce. Garnish with parsley sprigs and serve immediately.

monkfish parcels

ingredients

SERVES 4

4 tsp olive oil

2 courgettes, sliced

1 large red pepper, peeled, deseeded and cut into strips

2 monkfish fillets, about 125 g/ 4$\frac{1}{2}$ oz each, skin and membrane removed

6 smoked streaky bacon rashers

salt and pepper

freshly cooked pasta and olive bread, to serve

method

1 Preheat the oven to 190°C/375°F/Gas Mark 5. Cut 4 large pieces of foil, each about 23 cm/ 9 inches square. Brush them lightly with a little of the oil, then divide the courgettes and red pepper among them.

2 Rinse the fish fillets under cold running water and pat dry with kitchen paper. Cut them in half, then put 1 piece on top of each pile of courgettes and pepper. Cut the bacon rashers in half and lay 3 pieces across each piece of fish. Season to taste with salt and pepper, drizzle over the remaining oil and close up the parcels. Seal tightly, transfer to an ovenproof dish and bake in the preheated oven for 25 minutes.

3 Remove from the oven, open each foil parcel slightly and serve with cooked pasta and olive bread.

spicy monkfish rice

ingredients

SERVES 4

1 fresh hot red chilli,
   deseeded and chopped

1 tsp chilli flakes

2 garlic cloves, chopped

pinch of saffron

3 tbsp roughly chopped fresh
   mint leaves, plus extra
   to garnish

4 tbsp olive oil

2 tbsp lemon juice

350 g/12 oz monkfish fillet,
   cut into bite-sized pieces

1 onion, finely chopped

225 g/8 oz long-grain rice

400g/14 oz canned chopped
   tomatoes

200 ml/7 fl oz coconut milk

115 g/4 oz peas

salt and pepper

method

1 Process the chilli, chilli flakes, garlic, saffron, mint, oil and lemon juice in a food processor or blender until combined, but not smooth.

2 Put the monkfish into a non-metallic dish and pour over the spice paste, turning to coat. Cover and set aside for 20 minutes to marinate.

3 Heat a large pan until very hot. Using a slotted spoon, lift the monkfish from the marinade and add, in batches, to the hot pan. Cook for 3–4 minutes, until browned and firm. Remove with a slotted spoon and set aside.

4 Add the onion and remaining marinade to the pan and cook for 5 minutes, until softened and lightly browned. Add the rice and stir until well coated. Add the tomatoes and coconut milk. Bring to the boil, cover and simmer very gently for 15 minutes.

5 Stir in the peas, season to taste with salt and pepper and arrange the fish over the top. Cover and continue to cook over a very low heat for 5 minutes. Serve garnished with the chopped mint.

vegetables & pulses

It could be said that vegetables are the perfect choice for one-pot cooking as there is such an enormous variety and they go so well together. They're also great combined with pulses, providing a well-balanced, healthy and, of course, flavoursome meal. Whether you're using fresh-tasting baby vegetables in the spring, filling and satisfying roots in the winter or the sun-ripened harvest of the summer, the options are almost endless and there is sure to be a dish to suit everyone. Even those who claim not to like vegetables will be pleasantly surprised by how delicious they taste when they are cooked together in a mouth-watering one-pot medley.

Vegetarian stews and casseroles can be either warming and substantial or more delicate and subtle, and have the added advantage of requiring less cooking time than their meat-based counterparts. Other one-pot techniques are usually even quicker and vegetables are great stir-fried, roasted and baked, as well as combined in curries, risottos and pilaus. With these tasty options, you save not only time but money too, as they are very economical. There's every reason to include a one-pot vegetarian dish in the family menu occasionally even if you eat meat the rest of the time. Whichever recipe you choose, eating more vegetables has never been more enjoyable.

italian vegetable stew

ingredients

SERVES 4

4 garlic cloves

1 small acorn squash,
      deseeded and peeled

1 red onion, sliced

2 leeks, sliced

1 aubergine, sliced

1 small celeriac, diced

2 turnips, sliced

2 plum tomatoes, chopped

1 carrot, sliced

1 courgette, sliced

2 red peppers, deseeded and
      chopped

1 fennel bulb, sliced

175 g/6 oz chard, chopped

2 bay leaves

$1/2$ tsp fennel seeds

$1/2$ tsp chilli powder

pinch each of dried thyme,
      dried oregano and sugar

125 ml/4 fl oz extra virgin
      olive oil

225 ml/8 fl oz vegetable stock

25 g/1 oz fresh basil leaves,
      torn

4 tbsp chopped fresh parsley

salt and pepper

2 tbsp freshly grated
      Parmesan cheese,
      to garnish

method

1 Finely chop the garlic and dice the squash. Put them in a large heavy-based saucepan with a tight-fitting lid. Add the onion, leeks, aubergine, celeriac, turnips, tomatoes, carrot, courgette, red peppers, fennel, chard, bay leaves, fennel seeds, chilli powder, thyme, oregano, sugar, oil, stock and half the basil. Mix together well, then bring to the boil.

2 Reduce the heat, cover and simmer for 30 minutes, or until all the vegetables are tender.

3 Sprinkle in the remaining basil and the parsley and season to taste with salt and pepper. Serve immediately, sprinkled with cheese.

spring stew

ingredients

SERVES 4

2 tbsp olive oil

4–8 baby onions, halved

2 celery sticks, cut into
5-mm/^{1}/$_4$-inch slices

225 g/8 oz baby carrots,
scrubbed, and halved
if large

300 g/10^1/$_2$ oz new potatoes,
scrubbed and halved,
or quartered if large

850 ml–1.2 litres/1^1/$_2$–2 pints
vegetable stock

400 g/14 oz canned haricot
beans, drained and rinsed

1 fresh bouquet garni

1^1/$_2$–2 tbsp light soy sauce

85 g/3 oz baby corn

115 g/4 oz frozen or shelled
fresh broad beans, thawed
if frozen

^{1}/$_2$–1 Savoy or spring
cabbage, about 225 g/8 oz

1^1/$_2$ tbsp cornflour

2 tbsp cold water

salt and pepper

55–85 g/2–3 oz Parmesan or
mature Cheddar cheese,
grated, to serve

method

1 Heat the oil in a large heavy-based saucepan with a tight-fitting lid. Add the onions, celery, carrots and potatoes and cook, stirring frequently, for 5 minutes, or until softened. Add the stock, drained beans, bouquet garni and soy sauce, then bring to the boil. Reduce the heat, cover and simmer for 12 minutes.

2 Add the baby corn and broad beans and season to taste with salt and pepper. Simmer for a further 3 minutes.

3 Meanwhile, discard the outer leaves and hard central core from the cabbage and shred the leaves. Add to the saucepan and simmer for a further 3–5 minutes, or until all the vegetables are tender.

4 Blend the cornflour with the water, stir into the stew and cook, stirring, for 4–6 minutes, or until the liquid has thickened. Serve with grated cheese, to stir into the stew.

tuscan bean stew

ingredients

SERVES 4

1 large fennel bulb

2 tbsp olive oil

1 red onion, cut into small
    wedges

2–4 garlic cloves, sliced

1 fresh green chilli, deseeded
    and chopped

1 small aubergine, about
    225 g/8 oz, cut into chunks

2 tbsp tomato purée

450–600 ml/16 fl oz–1 pint
    vegetable stock

450 g/1 lb ripe tomatoes

1 tbsp balsamic vinegar

a few fresh oregano sprigs

400 g/14 oz canned borlotti
    beans

400 g/14 oz canned flageolet
    beans

1 yellow pepper, deseeded
    and cut into small strips

1 courgette, sliced into half
    moons

55 g/2 oz stoned black olives

25 g/1 oz fresh Parmesan
    cheese shavings

salt and pepper

crusty bread, to serve

method

1 Trim the fennel and reserve any feathery fronds, then cut the bulb into small strips. Heat the oil in a large heavy-based saucepan with a tight-fitting lid and cook the onion, garlic, chilli and fennel strips, stirring frequently, for 5–8 minutes, or until softened.

2 Add the aubergine and cook, stirring frequently, for 5 minutes. Blend the tomato purée with a little of the stock in a jug and pour over the fennel mixture, then add the remaining stock, the tomatoes, vinegar and oregano. Bring to the boil, then reduce the heat, cover and simmer for 15 minutes, or until the tomatoes have begun to collapse.

3 Drain and rinse the beans, then drain again. Add them to the pan with the yellow pepper, courgette and olives. Simmer for a further 15 minutes, or until all the vegetables are tender. Taste and adjust the seasoning. Scatter with the Parmesan cheese shavings and serve garnished with the reserved fennel fronds, accompanied by crusty bread.

potato & lemon casserole

ingredients

SERVES 4

100 ml/3^1/$_2$ fl oz olive oil

2 red onions, cut into
    8 wedges

3 garlic cloves, crushed

2 tsp ground cumin

2 tsp ground coriander

pinch of cayenne pepper

1 carrot, thickly sliced

2 small turnips, quartered

1 courgette, sliced

500 g/1 lb 2 oz potatoes,
    thickly sliced

juice and grated rind of
    2 large lemons

300 ml/10 fl oz vegetable
    stock

2 tbsp chopped fresh
    coriander

salt and pepper

method

1 Heat the oil in a flameproof casserole. Add the onions and sauté over a medium heat, stirring frequently, for 3 minutes.

2 Add the garlic and cook for 30 seconds. Stir in the ground cumin, ground coriander and cayenne and cook, stirring constantly, for 1 minute.

3 Add the carrot, turnips, courgette and potatoes and stir to coat in the oil.

4 Add the lemon juice and rind and the stock. Season to taste with salt and pepper. Cover and cook over a medium heat, stirring occasionally, for 20–30 minutes, until tender.

5 Remove the lid, sprinkle in the chopped fresh coriander and stir well. Serve immediately.

lentil & rice casserole

ingredients

SERVES 4

225 g/8 oz red lentils

55 g/2 oz long-grain rice

1.2 litres/2 pints vegetable
stock

1 leek, cut into chunks

3 garlic cloves, crushed

400 g/14 oz canned chopped
tomatoes

1 tsp ground cumin

1 tsp chilli powder

1 tsp garam masala

1 red pepper, deseeded
and sliced

100 g/3$^{1}/_{2}$ oz small broccoli
florets

8 baby corn, halved
lengthways

55 g/2 oz French beans,
halved

1 tbsp shredded fresh basil,
plus extra sprigs to garnish

salt and pepper

method

1 Place the lentils, rice and stock in a large flameproof casserole and cook over a low heat, stirring occasionally, for 20 minutes.

2 Add the leek, garlic, tomatoes and their can juices, ground cumin, chilli powder, garam masala, red pepper, broccoli, baby corn and French beans to the pan.

3 Bring the mixture to the boil, reduce the heat, cover and simmer for a further 10–15 minutes, or until the vegetables are tender.

4 Add the shredded basil and season to taste with salt and pepper. Garnish with basil sprigs and serve immediately.

vegetable goulash

ingredients

SERVES 4

15 g/¹/₂ oz sun-dried
    tomatoes, chopped

2 tbsp olive oil

¹/₂–1 tsp crushed dried
    chillies

2–3 garlic cloves, chopped

1 large onion, cut into small
    wedges

1 small celeriac, cut into
    small chunks

225 g/8 oz carrots, sliced

225 g/8 oz new potatoes,
    scrubbed and cut into
    chunks

1 small acorn squash,
    deseeded, peeled and
    cut into small chunks,
    about 225 g/8 oz
    prepared weight

2 tbsp tomato purée

300 ml/10 fl oz vegetable
    stock

450 g/1 lb canned Puy
    or green lentils, drained
    and rinsed

1–2 tsp hot paprika

a few fresh thyme sprigs

450 g/1 lb ripe tomatoes

soured cream and crusty
    bread, to serve

method

1 Put the sun-dried tomatoes in a small heatproof bowl, cover with almost-boiling water and leave to soak for 15–20 minutes. Drain, reserving the soaking liquid.

2 Heat the oil in a large heavy-based saucepan with a tight-fitting lid and cook the chillies, garlic, onion, celeriac, carrots, potatoes and squash, stirring frequently, for 5–8 minutes, until softened.

3 Blend the tomato purée with a little of the stock in a jug and pour over the vegetable mixture, then add the remaining stock, lentils, the sun-dried tomatoes and their soaking liquid, the paprika and thyme.

4 Bring to the boil, then reduce the heat, cover and simmer for 15 minutes. Add the fresh tomatoes and simmer for a further 15 minutes, or until the vegetables and lentils are tender. Serve topped with spoonfuls of soured cream and accompanied by crusty bread.

vegetable chilli

ingredients

SERVES 4

1 aubergine, peeled if wished,
    cut into 2.5-cm/1-inch
    slices
1 tbsp olive oil, plus extra
    for brushing
1 large red or yellow onion,
    finely chopped
2 red or yellow peppers,
    deseeded and finely
    chopped
3–4 garlic cloves, finely
    chopped or crushed
800 g/1 lb 12 oz canned
    chopped tomatoes
1 tbsp mild chilli powder,
    or to taste
1/2 tsp ground cumin
1/2 tsp dried oregano
2 small courgettes, quartered
    lengthways and sliced
400 g/14 oz canned kidney
    beans, drained and rinsed
450 ml/16 fl oz water
1 tbsp tomato purée
salt and pepper
chopped spring onions and
    grated Cheddar cheese,
    to serve

method

1 Brush the aubergine slices on 1 side with oil. Heat half the oil in a large heavy-based frying pan over a medium–high heat. Add the aubergine slices, oiled side up, and cook for 5–6 minutes, until browned on 1 side. Turn the slices over, cook on the other side until browned and transfer to a plate. Cut into bite-sized pieces.

2 Heat the remaining oil in a large saucepan over a medium heat. Add the onion and peppers and cook, stirring occasionally, for 3–4 minutes, until the onion is just softened but not browned. Add the garlic and continue cooking for 2–3 minutes, or until the onion is just beginning to colour.

3 Add the tomatoes, chilli powder, cumin and oregano. Season to taste with salt and pepper. Bring just to the boil, reduce the heat, cover and simmer gently for 15 minutes.

4 Add the courgettes, aubergine and beans. Stir in the water and the tomato purée. Bring back to the boil, then cover the pan and continue simmering for about 45 minutes, or until the vegetables are tender. Taste and then adjust the seasoning if necessary. If you prefer a hotter dish, stir in a little more chilli powder.

5 Ladle into warmed bowls and top with spring onions and cheese.

spicy chickpea & aubergine casserole

ingredients

SERVES 6

1 tbsp cumin seeds

2 tbsp coriander seeds

2 tsp dried oregano or thyme

5 tbsp vegetable oil

2 onions, chopped

1 red pepper, deseeded and cut into 2-cm/³/4-inch chunks

1 aubergine, cut into 2-cm/³/4-inch chunks

2 garlic cloves, chopped

1 fresh green chilli, chopped

400 g/14 oz canned chopped tomatoes

400 g/14 oz canned chickpeas, drained and rinsed

225 g/8 oz green beans, cut into 2-cm/³/4-inch lengths

600 ml/1 pint stock

3 tbsp chopped fresh coriander

method

1 Dry-fry the seeds in a heavy-based frying pan for a few seconds, until aromatic. Add the oregano and cook for a further few seconds. Remove from the heat, transfer to a mortar and crush with a pestle.

2 Heat the oil in a large heavy-based casserole dish. Cook the onions, red pepper and aubergine for 10 minutes, until soft. Add the ground seed mixture, garlic and chilli and cook for a further 2 minutes.

3 Add the tomatoes, chickpeas, green beans and stock. Bring to the boil, then cover and simmer gently for 1 hour. Stir in the coriander and serve immediately.

moroccan vegetable stew

ingredients

SERVES 4

2 tbsp olive oil

1 Spanish onion, finely
chopped

2–4 garlic cloves, crushed

1 fresh red chilli, deseeded
and sliced

1 aubergine, about 225 g/
8 oz, cut into small chunks

small piece fresh ginger,
peeled and grated

1 tsp ground cumin

1 tsp ground coriander

pinch of saffron threads or
1/2 tsp turmeric

1–2 cinnamon sticks

1/2–1 butternut squash,
about 450 g/1 lb, peeled,
deseeded and cut into
small chunks

225 g/8 oz sweet potatoes,
cut into small chunks

85 g/3 oz ready-to-eat prunes

450–600 ml/16 fl oz–1 pint
vegetable stock

4 tomatoes, chopped

400 g/14 oz canned
chickpeas, drained
and rinsed

1 tbsp chopped fresh
coriander, to garnish

method

1 Heat the oil in a large heavy-based saucepan
with a tight-fitting lid and cook the onion, garlic,
chilli and aubergine, stirring frequently,
for 5–8 minutes, until softened.

2 Add the ginger, cumin, ground coriander
and saffron and cook, stirring constantly,
for 2 minutes. Bruise the cinnamon stick.

3 Add the cinnamon, squash, sweet potatoes,
prunes, stock and tomatoes to the saucepan
and bring to the boil. Reduce the heat,
cover and simmer, stirring occasionally,
for 20 minutes. Add the chickpeas to the
saucepan and cook for a further 10 minutes.
Discard the cinnamon stick and serve
garnished with the fresh coriander.

chilli bean stew

ingredients

SERVES 4–6

2 tbsp olive oil

1 onion, chopped

2–4 garlic cloves, chopped

2 fresh red chillies, deseeded
   and sliced

225 g/8 oz canned kidney
   beans, drained and rinsed

225 g/8 oz canned cannellini
   beans, drained and rinsed

225 g/8 oz canned chickpeas,
   drained and rinsed

1 tbsp tomato purée

700–850 ml/1^1/$_4$–1^1/$_2$ pints
   vegetable stock

1 red pepper, deseeded and
   chopped

4 tomatoes, roughly chopped

175 g/6 oz frozen or shelled
   fresh broad beans, thawed
   if frozen

1 tbsp chopped fresh
   coriander, plus extra
   to garnish

pepper

soured cream, to serve

paprika, to garnish

method

1 Heat the oil in a large heavy-based saucepan
with a tight-fitting lid and cook the onion,
garlic and chillies, stirring frequently, for
5 minutes, or until softened. Add the kidney
beans, cannellini beans and chickpeas.
Blend the tomato purée with a little of the
stock in a jug and pour over the bean mixture,
then add the remaining stock. Bring to the
boil, then reduce the heat and simmer for
10–15 minutes.

2 Add the red pepper, tomatoes, broad beans,
and pepper to taste and simmer for a further
15–20 minutes, or until all the vegetables are
tender. Stir in the chopped coriander.

3 Serve the stew topped with spoonfuls of
soured cream and garnished with chopped
coriander and a pinch of paprika.

roast summer vegetables

ingredients

SERVES 4

1 fennel bulb

2 red onions

2 beef tomatoes

1 aubergine

2 courgettes

1 yellow pepper, deseeded

1 red pepper, deseeded

1 orange pepper, deseeded

2 tbsp olive oil

4 garlic cloves

4 fresh rosemary sprigs

pepper

crusty bread, to serve
(optional)

method

1 Preheat the oven to 200°C/400°F/Gas Mark 6. Cut the fennel, onions and tomatoes into wedges. Thickly slice the aubergine and courgettes. Cut the peppers into chunks.

2 Brush a large ovenproof dish with a little of the oil. Arrange the prepared vegetables in the dish and tuck the garlic cloves and rosemary sprigs among them. Drizzle with the remaining oil and season to taste with plenty of freshly ground black pepper.

3 Roast the vegetables in the preheated oven for 20–25 minutes, turning once, until they are tender and beginning to turn golden brown.

4 Serve the vegetables straight from the dish or transfer to a warmed serving platter. Serve immediately, with crusty bread, if you like, to mop up the juices.

ratatouille

ingredients

SERVES 4

2 aubergines

4 courgettes

2 yellow peppers

2 red peppers

2 onions

2 garlic cloves

150 ml/5 fl oz olive oil

1 bouquet garni

3 large tomatoes, peeled,
    deseeded and roughly
    chopped

salt and pepper

method

1 Roughly chop the aubergines and courgettes, and deseed and chop the peppers. Slice the onions and finely chop the garlic.

2 Heat the oil in a large saucepan. Add the onions and cook over a low heat, stirring occasionally, for 5 minutes, or until softened. Add the garlic and cook, stirring frequently for a further 2 minutes.

3 Add the aubergines, courgettes and peppers. Increase the heat to medium and cook, stirring occasionally, until the peppers begin to colour. Add the bouquet garni, reduce the heat, cover and simmer gently for 40 minutes.

4 Stir in the chopped tomatoes and season to taste with salt and pepper. Re-cover the saucepan and simmer gently for a further 10 minutes. Remove and discard the bouquet garni. Serve warm or cold.

butternut squash stir-fry

ingredients

SERVES 4

1 kg/2 lb 4 oz butternut
    squash, peeled
3 tbsp groundnut oil
1 onion, sliced
2 garlic cloves, crushed
1 tsp coriander seeds
1 tsp cumin seeds
2 tbsp chopped fresh
    coriander, plus extra
    to garnish
150 ml/5 fl oz coconut milk
100 ml/3^1/$_2$ fl oz water
100 g/3^1/$_2$ oz salted cashew
    nuts
lime wedges, to serve

method

1 Slice the squash into bite-sized cubes, using a sharp knife.

2 Heat the oil in a large preheated wok. Add the squash, onion and garlic to the wok and stir-fry for 5 minutes.

3 Stir in the coriander seeds, cumin seeds and chopped coriander, and stir-fry for 1 minute.

4 Add the coconut milk and water to the wok and bring to the boil. Cover the wok and leave to simmer for 10–15 minutes, or until the squash is tender.

5 Add the cashew nuts and stir to combine thoroughly.

6 Transfer to warmed serving dishes and garnish with chopped coriander. Serve with lime wedges for squeezing over.

aubergine gratin

ingredients

SERVES 2

4 tbsp olive oil

2 onions, finely chopped

2 garlic cloves, very finely chopped

2 aubergines, thickly sliced

3 tbsp chopped fresh flat-leaf parsley

$1/2$ tsp dried thyme

400 g/14 oz canned chopped tomatoes

175 g/6 oz mozzarella, coarsely grated

6 tbsp freshly grated Parmesan

salt and pepper

method

1 Preheat the oven to 200°C/400°F/Gas Mark 6. Heat the oil in a flameproof casserole over a medium heat. Add the onions and cook for 5 minutes, or until soft. Add the garlic and cook for a few seconds, or until just beginning to colour. Using a slotted spoon, transfer the onion mixture to a plate.

2 Cook the aubergine slices in batches in the same flameproof casserole until they are just lightly browned. Transfer to another plate.

3 Arrange a layer of aubergine slices in the base of the casserole dish or a shallow ovenproof dish. Sprinkle with some of the parsley and thyme, and season to taste with salt and pepper. Add layers of the onion mixture, tomatoes and mozzarella, sprinkling parsley, thyme, salt and pepper over each layer.

4 Continue layering, finishing with a layer of aubergine slices. Sprinkle with the Parmesan. Bake, uncovered, in the preheated oven for 20–30 minutes, or until the top is golden and the aubergines are tender. Serve hot.

cauliflower, aubergine & green bean korma

ingredients

SERVES 4–6

85 g/3 oz cashew nuts

1^1/$_2$ tbsp garlic and ginger paste

200 ml/7 fl oz water

55 g/2 oz ghee or 4 tbsp vegetable or groundnut oil

1 large onion, chopped

5 green cardamom pods, lightly crushed

1 cinnamon stick, broken in half

^{1}/$_4$ tsp ground turmeric

250 ml/9 fl oz double cream

140 g/5 oz new potatoes, scrubbed and chopped into 1-cm/^{1}/$_2$-inch pieces

140 g/5 oz cauliflower florets

^{1}/$_2$ tsp garam masala

140 g/5 oz aubergine, chopped into chunks

140 g/5 oz green beans, chopped into 1-cm/^{1}/$_2$-inch pieces

salt and pepper

chopped fresh mint, to garnish

method

1 Heat a large flameproof casserole or frying pan with a tight-fitting lid over a high heat. Add the cashew nuts and stir until they start to brown, then tip them out of the casserole.

2 Put the nuts in a spice blender with the garlic and ginger paste and 1 tablespoon of the water and whizz until a coarse paste forms.

3 Melt half the ghee in the casserole over a medium–high heat. Add the onion and fry for 5–8 minutes, or until golden brown. Add the nut paste and stir for 5 minutes. Stir in the cardamom pods, cinnamon stick and turmeric. Add the cream and the remaining water and bring to the boil, stirring. Reduce the heat to the lowest level, cover the casserole and simmer for 5 minutes.

4 Add the potatoes, cauliflower and garam masala to the casserole and simmer, covered, for 5 minutes. Stir in the aubergine and green beans and continue simmering for a further 5 minutes, or until all the vegetables are tender. Check the sauce occasionally to make sure it isn't sticking to the base of the casserole, and stir in extra water if needed.

5 Taste and adjust the seasoning, adding salt and pepper if necessary. Sprinkle with the chopped mint and serve.

vegetable curry

ingredients

SERVES 4

1 aubergine

225 g/8 oz turnips

350 g/12 oz new potatoes

225 g/8 oz cauliflower

225 g/8 oz button mushrooms

1 large onion

3 carrots

6 tbsp ghee

2 garlic cloves, crushed

4 tsp finely chopped fresh
   ginger

1–2 fresh green chillies,
   deseeded and chopped

1 tbsp paprika

2 tsp ground coriander

1 tbsp mild or medium curry
   powder

450 ml/16 fl oz vegetable
   stock

400 g/14 oz canned chopped
   tomatoes

1 green pepper, deseeded
   and sliced

1 tbsp cornflour

150 ml/5 fl oz coconut milk

2–3 tbsp ground almonds

salt

fresh coriander sprigs,
   to garnish

freshly cooked rice, to serve

method

1 Cut the aubergine, turnips and potatoes into 1-cm/$1/2$-inch cubes. Divide the cauliflower into small florets. Leave the button mushrooms whole or slice them thickly, if preferred. Slice the onion and carrots.

2 Heat the ghee in a large heavy-based saucepan. Add the onion, turnip, potatoes and cauliflower and cook over a low heat, stirring frequently, for 3 minutes. Add the garlic, ginger, chillies, paprika, ground coriander and curry powder and cook, stirring, for 1 minute.

3 Add the stock, tomatoes, aubergine and mushrooms, and season to taste with salt. Cover and simmer, stirring occasionally, for 30 minutes, or until tender. Add the green pepper and carrots, cover and cook for a further 5 minutes.

4 Place the cornflour and coconut milk in a bowl, mix into a smooth paste and stir into the vegetable mixture. Add the ground almonds and simmer, stirring constantly, for 2 minutes. Taste and adjust the seasoning, adding salt if necessary. Transfer to warmed serving plates, garnish with coriander sprigs and serve immediately with freshly cooked rice.

parmesan cheese risotto with mushrooms

ingredients

SERVES 6

2 tbsp olive or vegetable oil

225 g/8 oz risotto rice

2 garlic cloves, crushed

1 onion, chopped

2 celery sticks, chopped

1 red or green pepper,
    deseeded and chopped

225 g/8 oz mushrooms, thinly
    sliced

1 tbsp chopped fresh oregano
    or 1 tsp dried oregano

1 litre/1³/₄ pints vegetable
    stock

55 g/2 oz sun-dried tomatoes
    in olive oil, drained and
    chopped (optional)

55 g/2 oz finely grated
    Parmesan cheese

salt and pepper

fresh flat-leaf parsley sprigs,
    to garnish

method

1 Heat the oil in a deep saucepan. Add the rice and cook over a low heat, stirring constantly, for 2–3 minutes, until the grains are thoroughly coated in oil and translucent.

2 Add the garlic, onion, celery and red pepper and cook, stirring frequently, for 5 minutes. Add the mushrooms and cook for 3–4 minutes. Stir in the oregano.

3 Gradually add the hot stock, a ladle at a time. Stir constantly and add more liquid as the rice absorbs each addition. Increase the heat to medium so that the liquid bubbles. Cook for 20 minutes, or until all the liquid is absorbed and the rice is creamy. Add the sun-dried tomatoes, if using, 5 minutes before the end of the cooking time and season to taste with salt and pepper.

4 Remove the risotto from the heat and stir in half the Parmesan until it melts. Transfer the risotto to warmed bowls. Top with the remaining Parmesan, garnish with parsley sprigs and serve immediately.

risotto with artichoke hearts

ingredients

SERVES 4

225 g/8 oz canned artichoke
   hearts
1 tbsp olive oil
40 g/1½ oz butter
1 small onion, finely chopped
280 g/10 oz risotto rice
1.2 litres/2 pints vegetable
   stock
85 g/3 oz freshly grated
   Parmesan or Grana
   Padano cheese
salt and pepper
fresh flat-leaf parsley sprigs,
   to garnish

method

1 Drain the artichoke hearts, reserving the liquid, and cut them into quarters.

2 Heat the oil with 25 g/1 oz of the butter in a deep saucepan over a medium heat until the butter has melted. Stir in the onion and cook gently, stirring occasionally, for 5 minutes, or until soft and starting to turn golden. Do not brown.

3 Add the rice and mix to coat in oil and butter. Cook, stirring constantly, for 2–3 minutes, or until the grains are translucent.

4 Gradually add the artichoke liquid and the hot stock, a ladle at a time. Stir constantly and add more liquid as the rice absorbs each addition. Increase the heat to medium so that the liquid bubbles. Cook for 15 minutes, then add the artichoke hearts. Cook for a further 5 minutes, or until all the liquid is absorbed and the rice is creamy. Season to taste with salt and pepper.

5 Remove the risotto from the heat and add the remaining butter. Mix well, then stir in the cheese until it melts. Adjust the seasoning, adding salt and pepper if necessary. Spoon the risotto into warmed bowls, garnish with parsley sprigs and serve immediately.

vegetarian paella

ingredients

SERVES 4–6

$1/2$ tsp saffron threads

2 tbsp hot water

6 tbsp olive oil

1 Spanish onion, sliced

3 garlic cloves, minced

1 red pepper, deseeded and
    sliced

1 orange pepper, deseeded
    and sliced

1 large aubergine, cubed

200 g/7 oz medium-grain
    paella rice

600 ml/1 pint vegetable stock

450 g/1 lb tomatoes, peeled
    and chopped

115 g/4 oz button
    mushrooms, sliced

115 g/4 oz green beans,
    halved

400 g/14 oz canned pinto
    beans

salt and pepper

method

1 Put the saffron threads and water in a small bowl or cup and leave to infuse for a few minutes.

2 Meanwhile, heat the oil in a paella pan or wide shallow frying pan and cook the onion over a medium heat, stirring, for 2–3 minutes, or until softened. Add the garlic, peppers and aubergine and cook, stirring frequently, for 5 minutes.

3 Add the rice and cook, stirring constantly, for 1 minute, or until glossy and coated. Pour in the stock and add the tomatoes, saffron and its soaking water and salt and pepper to taste. Bring to the boil, then reduce the heat and simmer, shaking the frying pan frequently and stirring occasionally, for 15 minutes.

4 Stir in the mushrooms, green beans and the pinto beans with their can juices. Cook for a further 10 minutes, then serve immediately.